the pop classics series

national treasure.
nicolas cage
lindsay gibb

ecwpress

Published by ECW Press
665 Gerrard Street East
Toronto, Ontario, Canada M4M 1Y2
416-694-3348 / info@ecwpress.com

Editors for the press:
Crissy Calhoun and Jennifer Knoch
Cover and text design: David Gee
Series proofreader: Avril McMeekin

Library and Archives Canada
Cataloguing in Publication

Gibb, Lindsay, author
National treasure : Nicolas Cage /
written by Lindsay Gibb.

Issued in print and electronic formats.
ISBN 978-1-77041-236-1 (pbk.)
978-1-77090-760-7 (pdf)
978-1-77090-761-4 (epub)

1. Cage, Nicolas, 1964–. 2. Motion picture actors and actresses—United States—Biography. I. Title. II. Title: Nicolas Cage.

PN2287.C227G53 2015   791.4302'8092
C2015-902821-3   C2015-902822-1

Printing: Webcom   5   4   3   2   1
PRINTED AND BOUND IN CANADA

The publication of *National Treasure* has been generously supported by the Canada Council for the Arts which last year invested $153 million to bring the arts to Canadians throughout the country, and by the Government of Canada through the Canada Book Fund. *Nous remercions le Conseil des arts du Canada de son soutien. L'an dernier, le Conseil a investi 153 millions de dollars pour mettre de l'art dans la vie des Canadiennes et des Canadiens de tout le pays. Ce livre est financé en partie par le gouvernement du Canada.* We also acknowledge the Ontario Arts Council (OAC), an agency of the Government of Ontario, which last year funded 1,709 individual artists and 1,078 organizations in 204 communities across Ontario, for a total of $52.1 million, and the contribution of the Government of Ontario through the Ontario Book Publishing Tax Credit and the Ontario Media Development Corporation.

MIX
Paper from responsible sources
FSC
www.fsc.org
FSC® C004071

In Loving Memory
of Donald Kaufman.

Contents

Introduction

The first time I saw Nicolas Cage he was wearing a blue police uniform, calmly breaking up a fight between two drivers who had just been in an accident. It was 1994, and I was watching a VHS copy of *It Could Happen to You*, the loosely-based-on-a-true-story tale of a cop (Nicolas Cage) who promises half of his lottery ticket to a waitress (Bridget Fonda) because he doesn't have money on him for a tip. Then he wins. Cage is in his Jimmy Stewart mode: his soft, friendly police officer is the all-American nice guy, taking the neighborhood kids to play in Yankee Stadium, giving tokens to New York City subway passengers. This was decidedly not the film that converted me to the Church of Cage.

In 2007, I was working for a trade magazine publisher in an office made up of super-close-together cubicles that facilitated office banter. My workmates and I would debate various subjects like "'80s teen movies: good or bad nostalgia?" and "how old is the office carpet?" One day, the subject of Nicolas Cage came up. It seemed the general, easy consensus was that Nicolas Cage sucked. He chose bad film roles. He was a straight-to-video-caliber actor.

I wasn't sure I agreed. I had never run out to a theater to see a movie because it starred Nicolas Cage, but I'd hear that *Bringing Out the Dead* was worth seeing or that *Adaptation* was the new movie by the guys who did *Being John Malkovich*, and I'd go to see them. And they were good, and Nicolas Cage was good in them. The films started piling up, until I decided that Nicolas Cage was great in precisely six films: *Moonstruck*, *Wild at Heart*, *Raising Arizona*, *Bringing Out the Dead*, *Adaptation*, and *Matchstick Men*.

But with each Cage film I saw, I had to add another to the list. *The Weather Man. Valley Girl. Bad Lieutenant: Port of Call New Orleans.* Once I saw *Vampire's Kiss*, I became his great defender. In the face of co-workers belittling his oeuvre, I would retaliate: "Nicolas Cage is great in at least 10 . . . 11 . . . 12 films."

Having to constantly defend something you like can make you love it more fiercely. And being accused of liking something ironically was, at least for me, infuriating. (I don't have the time to spend hours in theaters watching movies I actually hate.) Soon I stopped tallying the films that proved Cage's greatness and my proclamation morphed into the declaration that Nicolas Cage is the best — and, more importantly, most interesting — actor in America.

The more I watch his films, the harder I find it to accept that some people have honestly concluded that Nicolas Cage is a bad actor (or even the worst actor of our time), but it's easy to understand how he's come to be treated as a joke.

If not reporting on his sensational real-life exploits, such as the legality of his dinosaur bones or the naked man he found at the foot of his bed eating a Fudgsicle, articles about Nicolas Cage tend to argue he is either the greatest actor or the worst. The result of Debate.org's "Is Nicolas Cage a good actor?" poll was an exact 50/50 split. He's been nominated for 10 Worst Actor awards at the the Golden Raspberries[1] and won best actor awards from the Golden Globes, the Screen Actors Guild, the National Board of Review, a large armful of international film festivals and critics associations and, of course, the Oscars. The internet is full of lists naming him the worst actor as well as the best; pop culture blog *We Got This Covered* ran an article entitled "10 Nicolas Cage Performances That Could Prove He's Either the Best or the Worst Actor Ever." In his life and in his movies, Cage confuses and confounds, eluding attempts to label him and put him in a box.

In the fifth season of *Community*, creator Dan Harmon used his pop-culture-obsessed character, Abed, to tackle the rich subject of Nic Cage. In one episode, Abed becomes obsessed with his class "Nicolas Cage: Good or Bad?" The premise is similar to the course Abed took in season two — "Who Indeed: A Critical Analysis of Television's *Who's the Boss?*" (spoiler: it's Angela). Abed finds the Nicolas Cage course so much harder to ace.

---

1 But he's never won!

Harmon was inspired to tackle the Nicolas Cage question because of the actor's ambiguity. The point of the episode, he said, was to confront the dichotomy of Cage: that he is both a good actor and someone who has done a lot of what Harmon calls "weird, dumb movies." And who better to be the unending-internet-debate stand-in than Abed? A staunchly unchanging and obsessive character, Abed expects to be able to reduce everything to clear terms to find a black-and-white answer. Instead, the Cage question made him modify his worldview because he couldn't put Cage in a box. (Or a cage, if you will.) Where Abed felt that actors could only be one type (good, bad, bad in a good way, good in a bad way), Cage was at least two things at once, and that blew Abed's mind.

Harmon articulated the confusion that surrounds our perception of Nicolas Cage at the *Community* convention, Communicon: "Nicolas Cage is a metaphor for God, or for society, or for the self, or something. It's like — what is Nicolas Cage? What is he? Is he an idiot? Or a genius? Can you write him off, or is he inexplicably bound to your soul?" Is Cage what the detractors say he is — an irredeemably bad actor, a joke unto himself — or what his devotees claim — "an actor of great style and heedless emotional availability" according to Roger Ebert, "the best living actor" according to me?

I understand Cage as an artist who is constantly reshaping and challenging audience perceptions of what "good" acting means; others think his face would look good on a Pokémon. These viewpoints are not unrelated. His expressive face is undervalued (and easily mocked) because he uses it in action, drama, and science fiction rather than just relegating it to goofball comedy. He broadens context, and we get confused.

Cage is experimental in the decidedly unexperimental terrain of Hollywood feature films. He looks to unconventional styles of acting (and even other forms of art) for inspiration. His disparate choices of roles are construed as a meandering, paycheck-inspired career,[2] rather than experiments with genre or proof that despite his singularity, and his notoriety, he can embody almost anyone.

When the easiest and potentially most successful career move would be to remain in genres that have been lucrative and critically respected, Cage instead chooses films that will make him uncomfortable and challenge his approach to acting. Just as his performances often take an unexpected, even uncomfortable, tack, he wants you to say "what the fuck" when you see the next movie on his slate. Never one to rest on his laurels or phone in performances, Cage consistently encourages viewers to question our assumptions and expectations about actors and acting, about art in general. And above all, he's always trying. And that's what makes him great. He's earnest even when it would be much cooler not to care.

---

2 In 2009, Cage owed $6.2 million in taxes. Critics will never forget.

1

Dualing Cages

"Right smack in the center of a contradiction — that's the place to be. That's where the energy is, that's where the heat is."

— Bono paraphrasing Sam Shepard, 1993

There are two Nicolas Cages. (At least.) There's the original — Nicolas Coppola, born into a large Italian-American family in Hollywood in 1964 — and there's Nicolas Cage as we know him: the character the young Coppola created to navigate the challenges of nepotism in Hollywood.

Nic took on the Cage moniker to avoid the attention the Coppola name drew. The nephew of acclaimed film director Francis Ford Coppola, he faced conflicting problems using his family name. On one hand, people expected him to easily get roles because his last name was synonymous with the movies, but on the other hand, he felt casting agents had higher expectations of him because of his celebrated uncle. At casting sessions early in his career, agents obsessed over his famous connections and wanted to talk about his uncle's body of work, to the point that Cage felt he was seen more as a representative of his uncle than an actor in his own right. Nicolas Coppola could never be certain he could get roles on his own merits, so he chose a new name — not a popular decision with his family. His father, a literature professor, wasn't happy that he wanted to be an actor at all, while Uncle Francis Ford was famously offended that Nic wanted to distance himself from the family name.

His chosen name had inspirations: comic book hero Luke Cage and avant-garde musician John Cage. "I thought [Cage] was interesting as it had two sides, the popcorn side and the more thoughtful side," said Cage in a 2014 interview with the *Independent*.

What Cage finds interesting — contradiction, duality — often confounds audiences and critics, inspiring polarity: inept/genius, best actor/worst actor, auteur/hack. This divided response has oftentimes reduced him to a punch line, but it's also arguably his greatest strength, enabling the breadth, diversity, and longevity of his career. Those who appreciated his "artier," more thoughtful work (*Vampire's Kiss*, *Birdy*, *Wild at Heart*) often feel he sold out with his action films, or the more popcorny side. Meanwhile, some moviegoers who know Cage for films like *Con Air* and *National Treasure* have no interest in *Raising Arizona* or *Bringing Out the Dead*.

In 1997's *Face/Off* and 2002's *Adaptation*, films that often make the evolving top ten list of Cage's best, the actor's duality is on very literal display as he plays two characters. In John Woo's *Face/Off*, Cage and his co-star John Travolta share the roles of the villain Castor Troy and the hero, Sean Archer. In Spike Jonze's *Adaptation*, Cage plays both lead roles for the entire film: twin brothers. Anyone who argues that Cage is one note, doing the same freak-outs over and over again, should look to his characters in *Face/Off* and *Adaptation*. While the films are extraordinarily different, in both the story follows the relationship between opposing and complex characters created by Cage.

In *Face/Off*, Cage starts off as Castor Troy, a terrorist for hire who, with his brother Pollux, has been dogging Travolta's FBI agent Sean Archer for years. Like many of the best movie villains, Cage's Troy is exuberantly diabolic. In the first present-day scene for the character, Castor Troy has just planted a bomb in the L.A. Convention Center. Cage, dressed as a priest, closes up the bomb cabinet and dances away, twirling and skipping proudly in his long black cassock. When he gets to the floor where a white-robed choir is performing Handel's *Messiah*, Cage claps, puts his hands on his knees, and head bangs heartily. Yep, he head bangs and struts to the *Messiah*.

Being "over the top" is right at home in a Woo film. Woo's work is highly stylized, often featuring extreme emotional juxtapositions, heavily choreographed shootouts, and elaborate clothing and weaponry. While his films are ultra-violent, they're also like a ballet. In *Face/Off*, these ballets are choreographed gunfights that take place on glass floors, set to "Somewhere Over the Rainbow," or during a high-speed chase featuring a speedboat as the stage. For Cage, working with someone like Woo — who wouldn't dream of stifling his imagination in the name of pure "realism" — is a perfect opportunity to stretch his abilities, playing both hero and villain in this heightened world of Woo.

Psychological turmoil abounds in Woo's characters once the film's central face-theft has come to pass: when Castor Troy awakens next to Travolta's preserved face flesh, Cage hacks, sputters, and shrieks a guttural birdlike squawk as he realizes his own face is missing. Later, when he's over the initial shock and straight into plotting mode, Cage-as-faceless-Troy smokes a cigarette and makes a phone call, using a muffled lisp that convinces us that his lips are missing. (Critics should pause: he is acting *without a face*, generally considered an important tool of the trade.) Cage remains staunchly committed to the absurd situation, and as a result, audiences buy in.

In a DVD commentary track for *Face/Off*, writer Mike Werb points out that while Travolta has to play two roles in this film (Archer and Troy-impersonating-Archer), Cage has to play three: Troy, Archer-impersonating-Troy, and Archer-being-Archer-in-Troy's-body. While Travolta's Troy enjoys the privileges and power of wearing Archer's face, Cage's Archer is horrified that he is trapped inside his enemy's body.

Even though Troy is such a fun character (in *Entertainment Weekly* Cage says he was playing him as the "Liberace of crime"), it isn't until Cage is playing Archer masquerading as Troy that the actor really shines. Second act Archer-as-Troy is confused, scared, and sensitive as he's shipped off to the sci-fi prison. The peak moment of Archer-as-Troy's inner turmoil hits when he beats up a fellow inmate to prove he is the volatile Troy. He screams in rage while he smashes his rival, then pauses between screams to cry.

In the same audio commentary, Woo explains that for him the most important preparation for a film is not the action sequences but the emotions of the characters. He likes to give his actors a lot of creative freedom. He gave Cage the freedom to decide how Archer would react to seeing himself as Troy for the first time. Cage improvised laughing, then crying, then smashing everything and yelling "fuck you" at everyone involved in putting him in Troy's body. For certain scenes in both *Face/Off* and Cage's second film with Woo, *Windtalkers*, Woo would set up three cameras around Cage to make sure they caught him from all angles, just in case he did anything unexpected. Perhaps the mirror-smashing, fuck-you-yelling scene is extreme, but so is having your face stolen. Cage and Woo work well together because neither is afraid to go out on that limb, experiment, and create a heightened reality.

As deliberately over the top and fun as *Face/Off* is, Cage's performance also includes moments of great subtlety. Take, for example, the scene where Archer-as-Troy visits an old friend of Troy's, a man who he's dragged in for questioning on multiple occasions, and in posing as Troy he must behave like this is a welcome reunion. When the friend, Dietrich Hassler (Nick Cassavetes), kisses him in greeting, Cage smiles through gritted teeth and accepts it halfheartedly, pushing him away before there's any chance to linger — Archer's contempt thinly veiled behind Troy's grateful embrace. When Hassler begins reminiscing with Troy about selling him the bombs because he "can't say no to a friend," Archer/Troy responds with a half-jovial, half-contemptuous "you drug dealer" in the same tone one might say "you old dog." Cage is acting on two levels simultaneously and manages to stay true to both characters.

Face/Off proved Cage's ability to be more than one thing at once, and five years later, Spike Jonze's *Adaptation* allowed him to go that one step further: he plays two characters, but this time opposite himself.

The film's premise is real screenwriter Charlie Kaufman's struggle to turn a book about orchids into a Hollywood motion picture. There's no drama or conflict in flowers, and Charlie wants to be faithful to the book (which, according to movie-Charlie, is written like "sprawling *New Yorker* shit") without injecting Hollywood clichés to make it more appealing. Enter a twin brother, the fictional Donald, who also wants to be a screenwriter and is more open to mainstream archetypes; he plays against Charlie's rejection of Hollywood's rules.

Here, Cage's duality — his popcorn side and his thoughtful side — is made flesh in Donald and Charlie. Donald is popcorn Cage, the actor who does action flicks, is dismissed as hackneyed by critics, but draws money at the box office.

Charlie is the thoughtful, artistic side of Cage who seeks out films like *Adaptation* that challenge audiences.[3]

Unlike in *Face/Off*, which Cage started filming three weeks later than Travolta because he was wrapping up *Con-Air*, *Adaptation* had a long rehearsal period before filming started, which allowed Cage to fully develop the characters and their relationship through improvisation. Cage's preparation and ultimate performance allows for the audience to instantly tell Charlie and Donald apart, despite similar hairstyles and modes of dress (. . . and the fact that they're both played by Nicolas Cage). Charlie comes with a furrowed brow, his unhappiness and anxiety written in his eyes. Donald has a light that rarely goes out, smiling more often and wider than Charlie, and he looks more inquisitive, while Charlie seems like he already has it all figured out. "Even at the first reading he had the two characters beautifully delineated," said Jonze during press for the film. "When Nic was Charlie he was a little more irritable and a little more difficult to direct. As Donald he was much freer and more open to suggestion. It really was like directing two different actors."

In a 2006 *Cineaste* article entitled "Performances in *Adaptation*: Analyzing Human Movement in Motion Pictures," Cynthia Baron uses Laban Movement Analysis (a multidisci-plinary method used to describe movement) to analyze the ways in which Cage makes Charlie and Donald truly distinct characters through physicality. Baron says that, as Charlie,

---

3 In press documents for *Adaptation*, Cage calls the film Cubist, after all.

Cage uses "pressing movements that are direct, sustained, and strong," meaning that he more or less pushes himself through the space. He hesitates more than Donald and only moves when he's sure of what he's about to do. Meanwhile, Cage portrays Donald's naiveté and carefree nature by using free-flowing motion, a style of movement that can "reveal vulnerability and convey a sense that a character approaches life not expecting errors or the need to adjust." In the press kit for the film, Cage explains that he did focus on the physicality of his characters before anything else: "I approached it from the British school of acting, creating the character externally and then working inward, rather than the Method school, in which you work from the inside out." Cage described Charlie as "morose, hypercritical, and joyless" while he saw Donald as "amusing, easygoing, and optimistic." For Cage, the key to initiating the differences between their movements was in the spine. Cage made Charlie hunched over and tense while Donald was more upright and loose.

Cage has demonstrated such mastery over movement and ability to convey character through physicality throughout his career. Cage is adept at physical expression and brings very specific movements to each of his characters. H.I. McDunnough in *Raising Arizona* moved like a real-life Wile E. Coyote; Terence McDonagh from *Bad Lieutenant: Port of Call New Orleans* is stilted because of a back injury that informs the character's entire personality; Eddie from *Deadfall* moves like an enraged Ed Grimley. Cage is great at going big, but he's also accomplished at using subtle movements to help him delineate his characters.

His physicality in *Adaptation* even translates in a motionless context. In a still used to promote the film, the two Cages sit next to each other in a hotel room. The Cage on the left reads screenwriting teacher Robert McKee's book; on the right, Susan Orlean's *The Orchid Thief*. Even though it is Charlie who is writing the adaptation of Orlean's book and Donald who is taking McKee's course, it is clear from just the still that Charlie is holding McKee and Donald is reading Orlean. Charlie looks quiet and contemplative and is clearly ignoring Donald, who leans toward his brother with something to say. Donald's eyes are wider than Charlie's. He's barefoot. Charlie doesn't seem like he'd ever be comfortable enough to take off his shoes, even when lying on a bed.

Perhaps it's Cage's attraction to doubled characters (and his own personal duality) that explains his affinity with Superman. Superman is one of the most iconic dual characters, and Cage — one-time owner of the original printing of the character's debut in *Action Comics* #1 and father who named his son Kal-El, Superman's Kryptonian name — almost was Superman in the late '90s. He was signed on to be the next Man of Steel in *Superman Lives*, written by Kevin Smith (later replaced by screenwriter Wesley Strick and then *Nightcrawler* writer/director Dan Gilroy) and directed by Tim Burton, which would have given Cage the opportunity to dwell on the psychology of being an alien raised by humans. If it wasn't for investors' "fear of trying something new, something that wasn't just more of the same" (which is how Jon Schnepp, director of *The Death of Superman Lives: What Happened?*, framed the film's demise in an interview with *Everything Action*), we would have seen Cage depict Clark Kent dealing with his alien status. Cage's Superman would have been emotionally torn between a relationship with Lois Lane and his anxieties around his identity, no doubt bringing hitherto unseen strangeness and depth to a character that we've only seen (on film) as the all-American hero. Perhaps we see a glimpse of what Cage had planned for *Superman Lives* in *Ghost Rider*. Superman's internal struggle would have been front and center, and in *Ghost Rider*, Johnny Blaze tries to run from his identity as a fiery creature before learning to accept and take control of his inner demon.

In these roles, as in Cage's film choices, it's not about one side triumphing over the other: it's about coexistence, not consolidation. Perhaps these roles get the closest to the fundamental reality of Coppola/Cage: he refuses to be reduced to an either/or proposition and instead embraces the contradiction.

2

Being Cagey

"Unless you're a total cynical dick, you have to embrace the fact that Nicolas Cage is a pretty good actor."

— Dan Harmon

Even though Cage is a man with a wife and children, like Jack Campbell from *The Family Man*, he is more often thought of as his character from *Drive Angry*: a man come back from hell who can turn the dial on his personality up to 11 at any moment. It's this (mis)perception that led to the label Caginess. Caginess (with a small "c") is already a word, meaning shrewd carefulness — a definition that is arguably the opposite of capital-C Caginess. Capital-C Caginess refers to a manic intensity that includes epic highs and lows, sudden outbursts of intense emotion, and surprise character traits (like Johnny Blaze's need to "drink" jelly beans from a martini glass and listen to Karen Carpenter before attempting to jump his motorcycle over six running helicopters). Moments of Caginess inspire people to compile clip reels of Cage's filmic outbursts, karate chops, and crying fits. This popular, punch line definition of Cage's acting style usually centers on one clip in particular: a scene from Neil LaBute's 2006 remake of *The Wicker Man* that isn't in the theatrical version of the film. Bees are poured into a cage on Cage's head while he screams, "Not the bees! *Arghlaglargh.*" Audiences mock this clip because they see it as Exhibit A in an earnest and failed attempt to remake a horror classic.

The film about a cop who visits a secretive island community to help find a missing girl is largely a punch line in movie history, considered a slap in the face to fans of the 1973 British cult classic. Rather than creating tension and unease in its audience, the remake generated confusion and laughter, particularly when Cage's cop dons a bear suit and punches a lady in the face. Audiences and critics see the film as a laughable failure, but there's no way that Cage and crew filmed that scene in particular — never mind the part where he drop-kicks Leelee Sobieski into a wall or yells, "How'd it get burned?" one or two times too many — without knowing the film they were making was a riot. In a 2013 interview with the *Guardian*, Cage said he'd wanted to play the cop with a handlebar mustache and a really stiff suit, which he feels would've made it clearer that the filmmakers were in on the joke.

Whether you like the film or not, Cage's character in *The Wicker Man* is emblematic of how we react when we don't understand what Cage is doing. Throughout the film, Cage's Edward Malus is striking out in frustration. He came to this island thinking he was doing the islanders a favor by helping them to find a missing girl, but instead he faces pushback from everyone he meets. By the end he screams and swears at children because he can't understand why they are resisting the help he's offering. Audiences, expecting an ominous horror film and getting an absurdist mystery, reacted the same way to *The Wicker Man*, and similar reactions plague so many of Cage's incongruous performances and choices.

We lash out at Cage because we're frustrated that he refuses to meet our expectations. Why did he impersonate Elvis in *Wild at Heart* and Adam West in *Kick-Ass*? Perhaps it's easy to say people mock Cage because they don't understand him, but there is a history of audiences reacting badly to art that they don't "get." In fine art, meaning can be even more difficult to decipher than in film. As psychologist Paul J. Silvia puts it in his article "Looking Past Pleasure: Anger, Confusion, Disgust, Pride, Surprise, and Other Unusual Aesthetic Emotions," an anger response to artwork can arise if a spectator finds a work "contrary to one's goals and values," and deliberately so. At the same time, a viewer who finds a work confusing may ultimately lose interest in that work because they find it hard to understand. This could explain why abstract expressionist paintings have been met with dismissal ("my kid could paint that" or "it doesn't mean anything") and hostility ("why is this worth millions of dollars?!"), and why the idea that Cage is making deliberate, if unconventional, choices in his roles is rationalized with excuses ("he's a hack," "he's lost his mind").

What audiences and critics who use the "Cagey" label seem to miss is that when Cage goes "over the top," it's not a mistake he makes while striving for realism. He thinks realism is overrated.

Realism is a stripped-down method of filmmaking that aims for authentic depictions of reality. Productions have a documentary look and feel, and actors strip away any stylization to create characters that just *are*.

In a 1994 *Los Angeles Times* article coinciding with the release of *It Could Happen to You*, Cage explains his choice to make lottery winning cop Charlie Lang a "larger than life" character: "Naturalism is a style that can be really effective, but it can be really boring."

And Cage is anything but boring.

This aversion to realism developed over time. Early in Cage's career, he was interested in fulfilling Hollywood's desire for reality, and he did so by method acting.

Method actors aim to create a character from the inside out. Tapping into the memories of a character for motivation, method actors often create a backstory for their characters and try to share their experiences offscreen in order to depict the character accurately onscreen. Known for more than just extremely detailed character development, some method actors lose or gain immense, perhaps unhealthy, amounts of weight for a role. (Christian Bale's skeletal character in *The*

Machinist is a particularly terrifying example.) Others stay in character throughout production and ask their co-workers to treat them like their character to help them really inhabit their role. (Daniel Day Lewis is well known for having the crew feed him on *My Left Foot* and living in the wilderness during *Last of the Mohicans*, and Val Kilmer once told Chuck Klosterman that he believes he knows what it's like to shoot someone better than people who have actually committed murder because he played Doc Holliday in *Tombstone*). Discussion of method acting often praises the authenticity of such lifelike performances, even if those performances took extreme dedication offscreen. (Extremity in the pursuit of subtlety — not un-Cagey.)

Two of Cage's earliest roles were in his uncle's films *Rumble Fish* (1983) and *The Cotton Club* (1984). In *Rumble Fish*, Coppola's second S.E. Hinton adaptation after *The Outsiders*, Cage played Smokey, a friend of main character Rusty James (Matt Dillon). Even though this was a bit part, Cage invented a huge backstory for the character. He figured Smokey wanted to be a businessman, so he picked up business textbooks trying to get into the head of his character. The pieces of inspiration he put together to build Smokey included Japanese management techniques, Iago from *Othello*, Machiavelli, and a lizard that bit him in a ditch.

By the time he was working on *The Cotton Club*, Cage's method approach had started to bleed into his outside life. Practicing to play a killer in his uncle's gangster picture, Cage embodied the character of wannabe mob boss Vincent Dwyer a little too well. He trashed his trailer and, on the streets of New York, he took a remote control car from a street vendor and smashed it to prove to himself that he could induce fear in people. (He apparently paid the vendor for the car afterward.) In 1984's *Birdy*, Cage played a soldier in the Vietnam War who, coming back to take care of his mentally ill friend, is also struggling with his own war wounds. To play a character who had just faced explosives in the jungles of Vietnam, he had two teeth pulled and wore a bandage on his face through the entire filming schedule, so he would feel more like a real war vet.

After making *Birdy* and *The Boy in Blue* (a 1986 film where he starred as a real person, Canadian rower Ned Hanlan), Cage began to bore of the method approach. He called his raw performance in *Birdy* "emotional vomit" and started taking roles where he could experiment with less traditional forms of storytelling. "I wanted to put back into acting a more surreal or expressive style that wasn't totally run by literalism, which seemed like a dead end," said Cage in a 1990 *American Film* profile. "I wanted to go totally in the other direction. And I began to realize a way that I could at once distort and reach a higher truth." He got his first chance to follow this desire in the third (and last) film he would do with his uncle, *Peggy Sue Got Married* (1986).

The film follows Kathleen Turner's title character, a woman who is in the midst of a divorce from her high school sweetheart (played by Cage), as she attends her 25th high school reunion. At the reunion, Peggy Sue passes out in front of her old classmates and wakes up back in high school in the

1960s. As such, all the main characters in the film have to play their older and younger selves, and Cage gets his first chance to play a dual role.

Cage interpreted the atmosphere of the film as taking place in a dreamlike state, and he translated that into his interpretation of his character, Charlie Bodell. Cage hadn't talked to the press much before *Peggy Sue*, but in 1986 he spoke to *Newsday* about his performance in his uncle's film because he felt that, like an opera, his performance might need a little preface to make sense to viewers. "In dreams, oftentimes, things are weird and distorted. So I thought, here was an opportunity for me to attempt some surrealistic acting," said Cage of his choices. "The reason why I come off as being weirder than the others is that no one else had that same perception as I did. So they are vertical and I'm sort of horizontal — going in a different direction."

His horizontal interpretation of Charlie, a high-school musician turned used appliance salesman, includes a high pitched, nasal voice that he got from Gumby's sidekick, Pokey. He sounds a bit like he's on helium. He also wore false teeth and cultivated an almost ghostly appearance with his pale skin and blond pompadour. Cage's interpretation of Charlie is compelling, though perhaps out of place in a film that approached time travel in the way most '80s romantic comedy/time travel capers did: like it was just a fact of life.

While Cage's idea to make Charlie surreal may have fit with his idea of the film, in the end he did it against the will of many collaborators. During filming, Kathleen Turner reportedly begged Coppola to kick Cage off the production because she felt he was making a mockery of the film. On visiting the set, TriStar executives were also unsettled and asked for Cage to be removed from the picture. Cage refused to change his approach and, to his uncle's credit, Coppola stood behind Cage's performance and let him go surreal.[4] In interviews after the film was released, Turner said that Cage didn't have the same structured approach to acting as she did, emphasizing her belief that he didn't plan out what he was going to do before filming a scene. This would be the first of many times Cage would have to defend his method. In his *Newsday* interview Cage said, "How can she tell what my method is? There was a reason for every little gesture I made, as awkward as they may have seemed at first . . . I went into the film wanting to try something new."

Surrealism looks at realism as a limited way of depicting truth. While realism favors interpretations that best mimic our outward visions of what is "real," surreal filmmaking uses dreamlike states to approach an inner truth that may look strange but does more than just approximate outer versions of reality. Cage, who worked with surrealist filmmaker David Lynch on his 1990 film *Wild at Heart*, felt that this approach was the way forward for him. "I think David Lynch's movies are more real than Spielberg's," said Cage in a 1990 *American Film* profile. "They're the inside reality. So I try to find the

---

4 Cage has said that if he had been kicked off the film and hadn't gotten the opportunity to take his abstract approach in *Peggy Sue*, he would've found another film in which to try it out.

film that will do those things, whether it's a dream state or just being insane."

As a child, Cage witnessed his mother's mental illness, something that drove him to pursue a more unfiltered, abstract truth. In an incredibly candid 1995 interview with *Rolling Stone*, Cage said that visiting his mother in institutions was difficult and frightening as a child, but he found his mother's visions to be very insightful, and the people he met in the institutions ("the characters," as he calls them) impacted his approach to his work. "If it wasn't for her, I don't think I would have been able to act," he explained. "I was just lucky that whatever was looking out for me gave me the ability to be a catalyst and to convert [the experience] into something productive. Since I was six I had invented an imaginary world where I could go to and be these other characters. That's probably where I started acting."

Cage's hyper-preparedness mixed with his increasingly experimental style led him to name his approach to acting "counter-critical," a response to critics who took issue with his over-the-top performances. He doesn't believe in "over the top." Instead, he believes in taking risks, trying something new, and working outside of the box. He feels that "over the top" suggests out of control, and to suggest that he has no control over the choices he makes with a character is simply untrue.

Peggy Sue Got Married began Cage's experimentation as well as his record of changing his style every few films. Just as his performance got mixed reactions from his co-stars and the studio, critical response was also mixed. In his review for

New York magazine, David Denby said Cage was miscast, and the *Toronto Sun*'s Bruce Kirkland said, "Coppola's grievous error was letting Cage (his nephew) indulge in his 'surreal' acting style (awkward gestures, a phony voice). Cage turns himself into such a monster it is difficult to believe someone as vivacious and bright as Peggy Sue ever married the creep." Meanwhile, *Newsweek*'s David Ansen called Cage an original, saying his Charlie had "surprising depth and poignance," and even though Pauline Kael thought Cage and Turner were mismatched and called the movie itself "sad crap," she had nice things to say about Cage: "Nicolas Cage isn't a facile actor; he works to get into his character, and he brings something touching and desperate to Charlie the small-town hot shot." Even though Cage's Charlie is a weirdly high-pitched and awkward cartoon character, he does truly seem to be affected by Peggy Sue.

Despite the mixed reviews his performance received, Cage longs for the freedom to approach more roles the way he did Charlie Bodell. "When I see retrospectives and that character comes on, it really lifts, you know, the mood of the audience. Part of me would like to somehow get back to that kind of — recklessness," said Cage in a *Rolling Stone* profile from 1999.

Cage's most successful roles are often about finding a director who supports his experimentation. After the actor's surreal turn in *Peggy Sue*, he attracted Cher's attention. She was so taken by Cage, she championed him to director Norman Jewison for *Moonstruck*. Cage started out butting heads with Jewison because Cage wanted to take a more punk-rock approach to his character, but Jewison steered him in a more operatic direction.

Consider the task of an actor in an opera: they must convince audiences that it is normal to be singing instead of speaking and, as in most stage acting, use large gestures to send emotion to the back of the theater. Everything must complement the enormous power of the singers, and big voices make for big drama.

Moonstruck is called operatic not because the actors are literally singing, but because emotion is king. Characters wear their hearts on their sleeves and expressions of feeling are heightened and immediate. In Cage's first major scene in *Moonstruck* he tells the story of his heartbreak to a woman he's never met before; you can almost imagine him singing as he calls for his assistant to bring him "the big knife" so he can slit his throat. To some this might be melodramatic; others call it operatic.

Structured to tell multiple love stories in one film, *Moonstruck* feels more like a play brought to screen than a typical romantic comedy. Director Norman Jewison took the operatic concept seriously, and even divided his cast up by their positions in the opera: Cher is the lyric soprano, Cage the tenor, Danny Aiello the baritone, Vincent Gardenia the bass, the aunt and uncle and grandfather the Greek chorus, and Olympia Dukakis the contralto. The tenor gets to sing the high note, and as Ronny, Cage hits emotional heights, serenading his wooden hand with tales of lost love and flipping a table when he finds love again. Yet Cage's performance doesn't seem inappropriate, since realism was never Jewison's goal: he even made Cage's character, Ronny, an opera lover as a hint to the audience.

Cage may seem like the obvious choice for such a role, but post–*Peggy Sue Got Married*, people were afraid to touch him. As Jewison put it in the DVD commentary, "The rumor around town was, 'Don't put Nic Cage in a film because nobody will come to see it.'" So when they were casting the Ronny role — which Jewison says was the most difficult part in the film — Cher and Jewison had to fight for him. After the first screen test the studio didn't want him, but Cher stood her ground and said she wouldn't do the film if she couldn't get "Nicky." He was the only person she could picture doing the part, and Jewison said he couldn't imagine anyone else having the "guts" to take on the role.

In a conversation with online interview magazine *The Talks*, Cage explained that he sees operatic and "outside the box," acting as part of a choice of how big you decide a performance should be. "I'm not the first one to do it," he pointed out. "In the '30s it happened quite a bit. Look at Cagney, was he real? No. Was he truthful? Yes." It's a theme that will come up again and again when studying Cage: realism isn't the only way to truth, as any opera lover would attest.

Cage moved even further away from realism next, with a style of acting he calls Western Kabuki. Japanese Kabuki theater has gone through a number of transitions since the 16th century, but its essential element is a collaboration of acting, sound, and physicality. Kabuki, an avant-garde style of dramatization, usually includes singing and dancing — more of the physicality and all-over performance Cage looks for. Composed of so many elements, Kabuki performances are equally a way for artists to exhibit their skills and a storytelling medium.[5] Kabuki performers wear makeup to exaggerate their features, and male Kabuki dancing is more like a series of elaborate poses that establish character than a dance.

Cage's mother, Joy Vogelsang, was a dancer, and though Cage never aspired to follow in her footsteps, he surely soaked up her way with movement: the way he jumps on the desk, points emphatically, and strides widely in a chase scene in *Vampire's Kiss*; the way he mixes martial arts with dance moves in *Wild at Heart*; the way he twirls, tangles, and slides in a claustrophobic fight scene with John Goodman in *Raising Arizona*. Cage even sings in some of his films (for example, he ad-libbed an a cappella version of a piece from Stravinsky's *Petrushka* in *Vampire's Kiss*, sang two Elvis songs in *Wild at Heart*, and made up his own songs in both *Leaving Las Vegas* and *Face/Off*). The way he regularly modifies his voice from role to role is perhaps a part of his Kabuki-esque approach. Describing Western Kabuki in a 2013 *Vanity Fair* interview, Cage said his goal was "to use my voice in almost a heavy-metal or operatic or baroque way."

This style, which he uses in films such as *Ghost Rider: Spirit of Vengeance* and, arguably, *Drive Angry* and *Kick-Ass*, allows Cage to emote with the seemingly limitless abilities of his face. Making these characters larger than life increases the

---

5 It's also fitting that Kabuki is passed down through generations of performers, since Cage himself comes from an artistic lineage.

entertainment value and, in the case of the *Ghost Rider* sequel, allows Cage to rise to the intensity of his directors, Mark Neveldine and Brian Taylor. Neveldine and Taylor are the duo behind the Crank films (the ones where Jason Statham plays a man who is basically suffering the same malady as the bus from *Speed*: if his heart rate slows below a certain BPM he will die), so naturally their *Ghost Rider* pushes beyond the original version Cage created in the first film.

When Cage re-evaluated his approach to Johnny Blaze in *Ghost Rider: Spirit of Vengeance*, he went to an acting style he dubbed Nouveau Shamanic, which involved integrating Afro-Caribbean techniques. For Cage, being Nouveau Shamanic meant sewing thousand-year-old Egyptian artifacts into his clothing, gathering "onyx or tourmaline or something that was meant to have vibrations," and painting his face white and black in a "voodoo priest" style to inspire him to be the Ghost Rider character. He explains that this technique is meant to trick him into believing that he is a character from another dimension with special powers. He doesn't say that this actually turns him into Ghost Rider, or that the artifacts or onyx have any real power over him as an actor. In fact, he says "who knows if it works or doesn't." Either way, it was a trick he used to help him believe he was the character, to freak out his fellow actors a little bit, and to turn up the volume on his performance as a man with a flaming skull for a head.

What all of these styles have in common is Cage's desire to experiment, to grow as an actor, to push the boundaries of what is comfortable, what is expected. Cage was not just honing his craft, but exploring its outer limits, even when those same borders were vigorously policed by critics and audiences.

In his 2013 Ask Me Anything on Reddit, Ethan Hawke said Cage is "the only actor since Marlon Brando that's actually done anything new with the art of acting; he's successfully taken us away from an obsession with naturalism into a kind of presentation style of acting that I imagine was popular with the old troubadours."

While the troubadours were known more for their lyrical poetry, the "presentation style" that Hawke describes carried over into theater and silent film acting. Actors from the earliest days of filmmaking used a style more akin to stage acting — filled with large gestures and extreme facial expressions — that looks exaggerated against today's realism. As film critic David Denby once put it, "Silent film is another country. They speak another language there — a language of gestures, stares, flapping mouths, halting or skittering walks, and sometimes movements and expressions of infinite intricacy and beauty." So much was conveyed without words, but it's a sign language of sorts that modern audiences have trouble understanding. Even modern films about silent acting (such as 2011's *The Artist*) tone down the grandness of this early style to make it jibe with modern tastes. Cage doesn't hesitate to use his facial and bodily dexterity, even though today it's criticized as bad acting because the movement away from silent film acting is seen as an improvement. Yet Martin Scorsese sought out Cage for the main role in *Bringing Out the Dead* because he wanted

Cage's inventive, expressive style, which Scorsese described as "almost like silent film, like Lon Chaney."

In her article "The Concept of 'Excess' in Film Acting: Notes Toward an Understanding of Non-Naturalistic Performance," Carole Zucker argues that the purpose of acting, or performance, is to convey words in a way that connects with the viewer or audience. She acknowledges the modern assumption that realism makes this connection best. However, in the case of film acting, isn't this connection dependent upon the way the words and emotions conveyed fit in with the world that is created onscreen? Using examples such as Jack Nicholson in *The Shining*, Crispin Glover in *Twister* (the 1989 one with Harry Dean Stanton, not the 1996 one with Helen Hunt), and Nicolas Cage in *Vampire's Kiss*, Zucker argues that the world presented by these films is heightened "or otherwise distorted," and therefore is "not bound by naturalistic behavior."

Cage's interpretation of Peter Loew in *Vampire's Kiss* is one of the clearest examples of his movement toward a presentation style of acting. It's also one of his best performances to date. In Pauline Kael's review of *Vampire's Kiss*, she says, "He does some of the way-out stuff that you love actors in silent movies for doing, and he makes it work with sound." The film, by British director Robert Bierman, follows a New York literary agent (Cage) who is struggling with life, power, and relationships. Cage plays a Patrick Bateman type;[6] a New

6 Though *Vampire's Kiss* came out in 1988 and Bret Easton Ellis's *American Psycho* wasn't published until 1991.

York businessman who is lacking control in one aspect of his life and is trying to compensate in another.

For the role, Cage plotted out his moves in front of the mirror before bringing his interpretation to the set, making a lot of specific decisions about the character's movement. When Loew is trying to exude confidence and antagonizing his secretary Alva (Maria Conchita Alonso), he channels Max Schreck (*Nosferatu*), moving slowly and elaborately through his office, stalking his prey, his head bobbing exaggeratedly back and forth. When he feels lost and snivels to his vampire master (Jennifer Beals), his movements are influenced by Peter Lorre (*M*), hunched, tight, and constricted. In a scene in his psychiatrist's office where he is ranting about organization and the frustrations of a misfiled contract, he rises off the doctor's couch and launches into his famous dramatic reading of the alphabet. This tantrum — in which he gesticulates wildly while firmly reciting his letters, clapping his hands, pointing angrily as the recitation becomes more and more intense — was one of Cage's most choreographed pieces, beginning with him stomping and pouting like a child and ending with a Mick Jagger–esque hip thrust. "Every one of those moves was thought out in my hotel room with my cat," he said in the audio commentary for the film.

Since *Vampire's Kiss* is not a silent film, Cage doesn't just play with movement, he also plays with sound and affects a British accent, or, more correctly, a sort-of British accent. The purpose was not to make Peter British, however. It was a class signifier, or, as Cage puts it, the "Continental bullshit accent."

Instead of indicating where he's from, the poncy accent helps to further explain the character and his insecurities. "I've seen people behave in that way, and I've always found it to be a big front, as though they were hiding something very vulnerable inside themselves," he told *American Film* in 1989. The accent belies these vulnerabilities that we discover in Peter throughout the film.

Zucker notes that while Cage's acting style in *Vampire's Kiss* is very self-conscious (Caryn James's *New York Times* review says that Cage's alphabet recitation scene, in particular, shouts "Look at me! I'm acting!"), "Cage's play with vocal intonation, highly choreographed movements, and stylized gestures provide no illusion of spontaneity. Rather, they are resources that exhibit the actor's special skills,[7] and speak to Cage's extraordinary level of competence, his 'bodily agility . . . control of facial muscles . . . and special verbal mastery.'"[8]

Over and over again, Cage is noted for his sleepy-yet-expressive eyes and the cartoonish malleability of his face. (Roger Ebert once said "No one can glance sideways better than Nic Cage.") He uses these assets, along with his lanky frame and highly controlled physicality, to combine opera and silent film–style acting, using exaggerated movement and emotions to create characters that keep audiences guessing.

In 1999, Nicolas Cage's colleague and one-time friend Sean Penn took a dig at Cage's experiments: "Nic Cage is no

---

7 Western Kabuki!

8 Here, Zucker is quoting from Elizabeth Burns's 1972 book, *Theatricality*, which links sociology and acting in order to examine the ways performance could affect its viewers.

longer an actor. He could be again, but now he's more like a
. . . performer." At the time, the criticism angered Cage, but
by 2013, in an interview for his film *Outcast*, Cage came to
agree with the statement. "When I act, I hear the dialogue
like music and the movement's like dance. So to me music and
dance are performing arts and, by the way, so is acting." He
designs his performances through movement before going on
set and then, in the moment, fills those performances with the
emotion of the character.

His performance in *Vampire's Kiss* is a mixture of the character overcompensating for the elements he feels he's missing
from his life, and his slow descent into insanity. While the
film ultimately has a "fresh" rating on review aggregator site
Rotten Tomatoes, the responses at the time were mixed. Some
critics claimed that Cage ruined the film with his "overacting."

Seeing "excessive acting" less as a reaction to or rejection
of naturalism than as a statement in and of itself, Zucker argues
in favor of excess as a legitimate style of its own, worth con-
sidering and defending. "The idea that acting for film should
adhere to a standard of gestural and psychological verisimili-
tude suggests a limited vision of performance," she writes.

And so, Cage in *Vampire's Kiss*, while perhaps more overtly
acting than in other, more naturalistic performances in his
career, is larger than life by design. In his counter-critical
style, he makes this character who torments and tortures his
secretary into something almost cartoonish so we can handle
the depravity of his actions. As Zucker says, it is a "challenging, exploratory style of acting" that asks the audience

to know they are spectators. By fighting against realism and inverting Konstantin Stanislavsky's rules about "learning to be private in public" (i.e., creating a scene that the audience feels its spying on), when Peter Loew eventually rapes his secretary, Alva, the audience can handle the disturbing action because there is no doubt that these are actors and this is a movie. This critical distance allows us to appreciate the performance without enjoying what the character is doing.

Cage's people told him not to do *Vampire's Kiss* because playing a man losing his mind and raping his secretary was not, in their minds, a good direction to go after the revered romantic comedy *Moonstruck*. But Cage wanted to do this, and Bierman stood behind the actor's choices. Perhaps Cage's performance seems "self-indulgent" in comparison to the rest of the film because Bierman kept most of the film naturalistic, but he did that as contrast to Cage's emphatic movements, to emphasize his increasing loss of reality. This was a considered collaboration, not an act of sabotage by a loose cannon actor out to see how much he could get away with.

Some critics did look favorably upon Cage's performance. The *Chicago Reader*'s Jonathan Rosenbaum said the real draw of the film was Cage's "outrageously unbridled performance, which recalls such extravagant actorly exercises as Jean-Louis Barrault's in Jean Renoir's *The Testament of Dr. Cordelier* and Jerry Lewis's Buddy Love in *The Nutty Professor*."

The film itself has been revived as a cult classic, and has received renewed analysis by the likes of the *A.V. Club* and inclusion in a retrospective of Cage's career at the Toronto

International Film Festival's Bell Lightbox theater. The *A.V. Club*'s 2012 feature on *Vampire's Kiss* describes the film as the perfect vehicle for Cage's talents. As the piece's author, Scott Tobias, says, "This film requires [Cage] to start at about eight and go all the way up to 11 — which is something Cage is fully capable of pulling off." While we see traces of Peter Loew in later performances (such as *Face/Off* and *Bad Lieutenant*), what Cage was doing in *Vampire's Kiss* was trying to get to a "new expression in acting," bringing German Expressionism — a high contrast, severe, almost cartoon-like style of acting and filmmaking popular in the 1910s and '20s, which famously rejected realism — into his style. Something, he admits, he may never get to do again.

With all of this dialing it up to 11, *Vampire's Kiss* is a prime launching pad for discussion of the meaning of "good acting." The question of whether Cage is a good or bad actor is on many critics' lips every time he puts out a new film. His back catalog is ripe for re-evaluation by film and culture writers, and the question is inarguably the key to the explosion of Cage as an internet meme.

Written by screenwriter Joseph Minion (also the author of Scorsese's *After Hours*), *Vampire's Kiss* allowed Cage to be absurdist, operatic, and method[9] all at once. Though he may not have been able to get away with this style in a movie where his character wasn't losing his mind, here, like the German Expressionists he sees as influences, Cage fully rejects realism.

---

9 This is the film where he ate a live cockroach.

In doing so, Cage crashes up against audience expectations and the norms of his own industry: approximations of reality are the performances most awarded by Hollywood's standards. Portraying a real person in a film is often the best route to an Oscar, and Cage himself is proof of that. His only nominations have been for approximations of real people: his character in *Leaving Las Vegas* (for which he won the Oscar) is based closely on the work's author, John O'Brien, and one of his characters in *Adaptation* is based on (and named after) screenwriter Charlie Kaufman.[10] But even in his depictions of real people (which Cage doesn't do often because he prefers to create new characters rather than emulate anyone else), he usually opts for a heightened version of reality.

"The day will come when naturalism will die," said Bierman when talking about stylistic choices in the audio commentary for *Vampire's Kiss*. "I think it's incredibly limiting because the best you can get is as close to reality as possible, and so many movies are really just trying to mirror reality. My thing is, then there is nowhere to go; there's no creative expression beyond it looking like a news reel."

For Cage, acting is the same as any other art form. "If you can get very outside the box — or, as critics like to say, over the top — in a Francis Bacon painting, why can't you do it in a movie?" he asked at a London press conference for *Ghost Rider: Spirit of Vengeance*. When Cage finds a film that suits his radical style, he often receives praise for his performance;

---

10 The winner that year was Adrien Brody for his portrayal of real person Wladyslaw Szpilman in *The Pianist*.

when he goes big inside something more toned down, audiences wrinkle their noses. This is perhaps why, when directed by filmmakers who understand the abstract (like Werner Herzog and David Lynch), Cage makes perfect sense.

Bad Lieutenant: Port of Call New Orleans (2009) feels built for Cage. Revolving around Cage's Terence McDonagh — an awarded cop who gets ornery and corrupt after a back injury leaves him hooked on drugs — the film's creative camera work (switching to hand-held at times to sit in a ditch with alligators and on tables with iguanas) adds an hallucinatory effect to the film and allows Cage to experiment with elated and confused facial expressions in the background while the camera focuses on the reptiles.

Herzog's *Bad Lieutenant* feels like the abstract painting that Cage had been looking for. Once again, he plays with movement and voice — he speaks through gritted teeth as he struggles with back pain; he uses a wheezy, maniacal giggle to punctuate his new, drugged-up persona; he walks with a stiff hunch and takes extra time just to turn to look at someone because of his injury.

McDonagh is Caginess incarnate. While memes tend to use manic outbursts to define Cagey, the nuanced darkness and light of the lieutenant — who is morally ambiguous, both corrupt and kind — show Cage's ability to be both a comedian and a villain. Calmly shaving his face with an electric razor as he stares down a little old lady is equally as unexpected as the joyful giggle he lets out every time he says the name of one of the suspected drug dealers: "G." Cage's range and energy are comparable to Herzog's former leading man Klaus Kinski. Herzog himself says that on camera they are two of the few lead actors he's seen with real charm. As Roger Ebert wrote in his review, Cage and Herzog make sense together because "they are both made restless by caution."

"There's a lot of things that make Nic unique," said David Lynch in an *American Film* profile of Cage from 1990. "His way of delivering lines, his look. He's got an ability to do real heavy things and goofy things. His attitude encouraged me to think of things for him to do, because he's so good at going into strange places. You give him an idea, and he grabs onto it like crazy. He's like a wild dog on a leash."

Lynch's films combine pop cultural references with surreal imagery, acting styles, and storylines, a combination that Cage thrives on. Lynch's dreamscapes allow for the kind of excess in film acting we've been talking about. In *Wild at Heart*, Cage's Sailor Ripley is bursting with physical energy. He dances with his raised arms extended and his legs karate-kicking the air. Even driving in his car, he salutes the road and bobs his head. His reactions to danger and sexual attraction are just as outsized, the former landing him in jail after he explodes and bashes a man's head into a marble staircase (the man was trying to kill him, but the reaction was a bit more extreme than expected) and the latter leading to almost endless moments of Sailor and Lula (Laura Dern) rushing back to their room to rhythmically writhe and thrust, always glistening as if it's 100 degrees.

Cage's Sailor may be big, but at times he feels like one of the most subdued characters in a film that matches his intensity.

He's surrounded by characters like Lula's mama (Diane Ladd), who paints her face with red lipstick and screams and cries in nearly every scene; Lula's cousin Dell (Crispin Glover), who likes to dress as Santa Claus, make sandwiches, and put cockroaches in his underwear; Juana Durango (Grace Zabriskie), a sadistic killer with a limp who wears wild hair and makeup and ritually tortures and kills her victims to terrifying music; and Bobby Peru (Willem Dafoe), a creep with tiny, rotten teeth, who is probably the most nauseating character ever put to screen. With all that going on, Sailor and Lula still manage to own the film.

Cage finds a perfect balance between the eccentric and the average, and there, Sailor is born. Once again going against Stanislavsky's rules — this time the rule that an actor should not try to imitate someone else — he used Andy Warhol's duplicates as inspiration and played Sailor as Elvis.[11]

Just as he brings absurdity to realism, he also grounds his surrealism in small, realistic moments. In *Matchstick Men*, Cage added a tic to his character's movements, in part because he knows people who suffer from tic spectrum behavior, and he wanted to say something about it by representing it on film. He also adds moments that are so real they're almost banal. Take shaving for example. Nicolas Cage's characters shave frequently enough in his films that I started counting the instances. There are nine that I've noticed. In a career of

---

11 In an interview for *Adaptation*, Cage said that if he'd known then that he would one day marry Elvis's daughter, he would've just played Sailor as Andy Warhol. That would've been something.

70 films and counting, shaving in nine films may not be a lot, but it's enough of a pattern to see what he's doing. In some cases the activity moves along the action, but most of the time it's a mechanism to make his characters more real. When Jack Singer is flying around the country trying to find his fiancée in *Honeymoon in Vegas*, he's so constantly on the road, he shaves in the back of a taxi. When he's debating what to do with his lottery winnings in *It Could Happen to You*, he's in the middle of a daily routine, shaving while his wife takes a shower. In *Bad Lieutenant*, he uses an electric razor while scolding an old lady, either because his character is on the job so much he has no time to shave, or just because Cage knew it would be a joy to watch. He shaves to give normalcy to abnormal situations.

When directors like Lynch and Herzog make surreal choices, audiences buy in. In large part this is because they've cultivated an audience around their respective styles, and Lynch in particular has created a dreamlike world that we expect to see each time out. Meanwhile, Cage receives criticism because his audience is splintered. He works within the world of each new director and often aims to find the absurdity in places viewers don't necessarily expect it. So when Cage plays more internal, realistic parts, critics breathe a sigh of relief. *Red Rock West* (1993) is Cage's highest-rated film according to Rotten Tomatoes. It's an example of critics taking Cage more seriously when he plays something closer to realism, in a way they can immediately understand and identify as "good" acting. But it's also a film that few people have heard of or seen.

In *Red Rock West*, Cage's Michael shows up in the small town of Red Rock looking for a construction job and ends up mistaken for a hit man. Cage spends a good portion of the film cautiously watching his companions as he tries to escape this ever-growing misunderstanding alive. The *New York Times'* Caryn James (who thought Cage destroyed *Vampire's Kiss* with his "self-indulgent" style) liked this toned down version of Cage. "Mr. Cage, once a champion over-the-top actor himself, has become more restrained, funnier, and appealing in the last few years (in films like *Honeymoon in Vegas*)," she wrote in her *Red Rock West* review.

Even Ebert, who was one of Cage's biggest defenders, seemed to like Cage's tamer side. In 1999, he praised Cage's role in *Bringing Out the Dead* (another quiet performance) as his best since *Leaving Las Vegas*. In this Martin Scorsese picture, Cage roams the streets of New York City, an insomniac paramedic who sees misery day in and day out, and you can see it all over his face. Everyone around him (his various patrolling partners, the cop who guards the hospital that is always overflowing with patients) uses their huge personalities to drown out and survive the constant torrent of misery. But Cage's Frank Pierce is quietly being killed by the city and the things its inhabitants do to each other. Even Joe Connelly, who wrote the novel the film was adapted from (based on his own life as an EMS worker), said that Cage embodied the role in a real, physical way: "You look at his face, and Frank's history is all there — what's going on in his head is right out in front of you." Much of this film is chaotic and dreamlike as Cage's

Frank roams the city night after night on nearly no sleep, but he plays the role as a quiet zombie instead of a delirious driver.

Most recently, in 2013, Cage decided it was once again time to strip off all the layers of "style" he had accumulated. He went after an opportunity to be natural in David Gordon Green's *Joe*.

Based on the novel of the same name by Larry Brown, *Joe* is a Southern tale about an ex-con who sees a bit of himself in a young boy who comes to him for help. The boy (Tye Sheridan) wants to work for him, and Joe endeavors to help this boy out with his family troubles, at great risk to himself. A slow, thoughtful cinéma vérité movie along the lines of the work of Terrence Malick — there are fields, and woods, and scrap yards, and much of the scenery gets the same amount of focus as the characters — *Joe* is quiet, and so is Cage's performance. Cage said that he sought out a role like *Joe* because he wanted to prove to himself (and in some ways, to his audience) that he could do something like this. While he's been pushing the limits of his craft over the past decade, this was an experiment in realism.

Cage is magnificent as Joe. Even though he's restrained in this role, Cage conveys the rage-filled man's emotions through his eyes instead of his actions. It's heartbreaking watching his eyes tear up with helplessness as he tries to keep his rage from boiling over.

The problem with Cage going naturalistic is not his performance; it's the reactions to it. Reviews of *Joe* called it Cage's redemption. Critics drew parallels between Joe's struggles with restraint and Cage's own "newly" restrained acting style. NPR's Bob Mondello calls his performance "more than a rescue — it's a rebirth." These reactions beg the question: does Cage have to cave to critical expectations of reality to get respect?

Cage may be considered bad if the definition of good is always realism. But as Nick Schager wrote in his *Vulture* article "Nicolas Cage Doesn't Need a McConaissance," to consider *Joe* his redemption is to erase "some of his best actorly qualities." His counter-critical style relies on going against the grain, after all.

Even when he's in a not-so-great film, he never "phones in" his performances. "He always seems so earnest," said Roger Ebert in his review for *Adaptation*. "However improbable his character, he never winks at the audience. He is committed to the character with every atom and plays him as if he were him." He's working as hard in *Adaptation* as he is in *The Wicker Man*.

Good or bad, Cage is happiest when the critics and his audience are affected by his work. If it's a choice between pleasing the masses or confusing them, he'll choose the latter. "What's the point in just getting good reviews?" Cage asked *Games Radar* in 2005. "At the end of the day, I want people to go, 'Well, what the hell was that?'"

3

Cage Against the Machine

"I can't get used up. It's not possible, because I am open to the world."

— Nicolas Cage

Nicolas Cage is a genius.

Genius is an overused descriptor, absolutely. It's wise to avoid calling anyone a genius just for being good at what they do. But Cage isn't just good at acting. He's created a career trajectory that baffles anyone who tries to follow it. When he seems to be staking a claim as an intense indie actor, he shows up in the mainstream comedy *Honeymoon in Vegas*. When you anticipate another romantic comedy, you get the darkly depressing *Leaving Las Vegas*. Or just when it seems he's become an action star, you get the sleepy and sickly Frank Pierce in *Bringing Out the Dead*. And when you concede that you don't even know what to expect anymore, you get *Next*, a film where he plays a magician who teams up with the FBI to stop a nuclear holocaust. The only thing that's predictable is his unpredictability.

The whole concept of creating work so unexpected that it throws off (and even angers) audiences is the premise behind Jason Hartley's Advanced Genius Theory.

Hartley is a writer and marketer, and he and friend Britt Bergman developed something called the Advanced Genius Theory at a Pizza Hut in South Carolina in 1992. The premise of the theory is that an artist is considered advanced if they follow a career path that falls into the following pattern: "early innovation that is not immediately appreciated, a lengthy fertile period leading to widespread acceptance, and a long (seemingly) fallow period that eventually sullies their reputations and angers their admirers." The pattern fits so closely to the trajectory of Cage's career, it's surprising the theory wasn't based on him.

The theory, which holds Lou Reed as its crowning example, requires any considered artist to have worked for at least 15 years and argues that artists who fit under this theory are often thought of as bad (or as having "lost it"), but have in fact continued to create amazing work that audiences simply don't understand. In his book *The Advanced Genius Theory: Are They Out of Their Minds or Ahead of Their Time?*, Hartley argues that "a great artist is great because he challenges himself and his audience rather than doing what is comfortable."[12] He points to Cage as one of these geniuses.

Like most people in his profession, Cage strives to take on new roles each time out, but as a movie star he's expected to find his niche and stick with it. Instead he offers proof of his abilities over and over again by taking on a wide variety of roles. Once again, Cage wants to be anything but boring, and his career trajectory is as emblematic of his ongoing war with convention as his character in *Peggy Sue*. The people who fit into Hartley's theory are considered geniuses of an advanced nature because they continue to challenge themselves to change even when staying the same would be the easier — and more widely respected — choice. Cage isn't a genius for being the perfect, wild-eyed H.I. McDunnough, and he's not a genius because of his convincing and Oscar-winning turn as suicidal drunk Ben Sanderson. Cage advanced when he teamed up with Michael Bay.

"Advancing . . . requires that the genius put aside everything that brought success and go down a solitary path, one that will cost him his fans, fortune, and reputation," writes Hartley. In fact, Cage's run through the sewers with Sean Connery seemed more like a joke or a one-off than a real move away from what he was known for. But then he kept running. "It came to pass that *The Rock* was by far the biggest hit of Cage's career, but we had every reason to expect Cage to cash

12 That "he" is telling: if there's a flaw in Hartley's theory, it's that female artists don't seem to be included.

his check and go back to the movies we loved him for. We did not expect *Con Air*."[13]

It's hard to look back at the roles he is now best known for and say this is where he made his most daring move. However, Cage was not action hero material in anyone's eyes before he made *The Rock*. He was a wacky character actor who was dabbling in mainstream fare. His rubber, expressive face turned him into the go-to quirky actor for comedies and weird dramas, and while doing one action film would have just been a weird departure, doing three in a row seemed like a whole career change.

It's because of his continued advancement that Nicolas Cage put out the widely lauded *Joe* followed by *Left Behind*, a remake of the religious rapture film series that originally starred Kirk Cameron (based on a book series by Tim LaHaye and Jerry B. Jenkins) that critics called terrible and worse than the original (which was also highly panned). Cage did *Joe* because he wanted to "be as naked as I can be as a film presence," and he did *Left Behind* because his brother, a pastor, asked him to. He's still keeping us guessing.

When it comes to Cage's style of acting, it's clear that he likes to try new approaches, and his choice of films has evolved and jumped around in concert with his attempts to find new places to experiment. But another reason Cage chooses a film, or switches genres, is to reach new audiences. In his review

---

13 A friend of mine asked Chuck Klosterman, an adherent of the Advanced Genius Theory, if he thinks Cage is advanced. He said yes, "categorically," specifically citing *The Wicker Man*, *The Weather Man*, and *The Bad Lieutenant* as proof.

for *The Rock*, late film critic Gene Siskel wrote that, when he met Cage at the Oscars, the actor told him his next few films would be "big-budget, action pictures" so he could build his commercial appeal in order to have the clout to fund "more adventurous, independent films."

Cage also felt that action movies were more universal than any other type of film. After filming the Second Italo-Ethiopian war flick *Time to Kill* (1989) in Zimbabwe, he noticed that the local people would gather together to watch Charles Bronson movies. He knew then that action films would be the genre that would deliver him to new audiences. Language barriers aren't as much of an obstacle when the film genre isn't particularly reliant on dialogue. In fact, in 2013 he was named Best Global Actor in Motion Pictures by the Huading Awards in China, and many of his most recent films have done over twice as well in foreign markets as they have in the U.S.

In an interview with Chinese Central Television (CCTV) while he was filming the Chinese period drama *Outcast* in China in 2013, Cage said he hopes to set up "a base" near mainland China so he can participate in the anticipated boom in Chinese cinema.[14] He wants to work outside the U.S. to learn from other cultures. "I want new experiences, I want to be stimulated to find new ways of performance," said Cage. "I want [Chinese] culture to find something in me that I have not found yet and will hopefully improve my work. I always want to learn."

---

14 He says he'll only get involved if the films have a need for "a white guy like me."

Even as Cage swerved into action movies, he didn't simply morph into action-figure mode. He continued to experiment with juxtaposition and with the unexpected, to try to do something fresh within the genre. In Bay's *The Rock* — in which Cage plays Stanley Goodspeed, an FBI chemistry expert called in to stop a group of Marines from bombing San Francisco with nerve gas — Jerry Bruckheimer and Michael Bay encouraged Cage to write his own dialogue and add his own ideas to the character. So he made Stanley an everyman. The everyman trope comes from medieval morality plays that see a character who represents all of mankind trying to correct his life so that he will have done enough good to make it into heaven. One of the earliest morality plays, *The Somonyng of Everyman*, is more specifically about approaching death alone with only your good deeds to represent you. In modern movies, the everyman is typically a character who is meant to make the audience connect with the story because they can imagine themselves in the character's position, even if the situation itself is unusual. This often means the character has no strong characteristics and is secondary to the story unfolding around them. Cage's characters are rarely without strong personalities; however, he's capable of playing characters that are relatable. In fact, many of his films play on the everyman archetype.

Like *Die Hard*'s John McClane and *Alien*'s Ellen Ripley before him, Stanley Goodspeed is an action hero who is vulnerable and shows fear instead of just being bulletproof. Cage was drawn to Goodspeed because it was his chance to flip the action hero on its head. He didn't buff up for the role (he was much smaller than he was as the thick-necked Little Junior Brown in *Kiss of Death*);[15] he created a character who refuses to swear (because he wanted the challenge and humor that came from finding other words to show frustration) and who cries when he sees someone die. He even vomits (and says, "My stomach's doing hula hoops around my ass") just before he heads over to Alcatraz to stop the VX gas from dispersing. Cage wanted his character to be an anti–action hero of sorts; a man who knows how horrible chemical weapons can be and is terrified of the consequences if he fails at his mission. The original scripted version of Stanley was a character who was thrilled to finally get an opportunity to get into the field, but Cage thought it would be more interesting to make Stanley a man who loved his job so much that he would be reluctant to leave the lab.

Cage believes the constraints of the genre also helped make him a better actor. "*The Rock* really taught me a lot about the style of the genre and what needs have to be met for it to work," said Cage in the audio commentary for *The Rock*. "It teaches you to be succinct, pristine in your choices or you'll get cut out." Everything an actor does must push the story forward because of how quickly the action genre moves.

In *Face/Off*, Archer is our everyman. He may be in the most absurd situation (stuck wearing someone else's face), but he's a relatable character because he's scared that not only will

---

15 At the time Cage also said he thought Stanley was a different kind of action hero because he didn't have a robot head, which goes to show what version of an action hero he was playing against in his mind.

he never see his family again but if he doesn't save them, they will be stuck living with a very dangerous man. While *Con Air* brings him a little closer to the typical action hero, complete with a requisite slow-motion-run-in-front-of-explosives shot and hammy one-liners to balance the carnage, he's still just a guy who wants to take a stuffed bunny home to his daughter.

Con Air's Cameron Poe (Cage) is the only good guy on a plane of mass murderers with the guts to single-handedly take them all down.[16] In a 1997 interview with the *Toronto Sun*, Cage likened his characterization of Poe to his approaches to *Raising Arizona*, *Red Rock West*, and *Wild at Heart*: "The manner is a combination of Elvis and Orange County monster trucks." He pictured the eighth grader he looked up to when he was in second grade: a guy working on his Chevelle in a cut-off shirt with a six-pack of Coors, and he played Poe as the adult version of that guy. The Average Joe who becomes the smooth action hero. And yet he's still not the action hero that was common before him. He isn't Stallone or Schwarzenegger or Van Damme.

If he expanded his audience with action movies, Cage took it even further with his move into the world of animation. As a father, Cage wanted to make movies his youngest son could enjoy, so he started making family-oriented films. He took on films like *National Treasure* and moved into voice acting in *The Ant Bully* (2006) followed by *G-Force* (2009), *Astro Boy* (2009), and the 2013 hit *The Croods*. Doing animated voices wasn't

---

16 Mykelti Williamson's character, Baby-O, is pretty much an everyman too, but he's too busy slipping into a diabetic coma to be the hero.

much of a stretch for Cage — he is already a cartoon in so many of his live-action movies, taking inspiration from Wile E. Coyote and Woody Woodpecker for *Raising Arizona* and Pokey for *Peggy Sue Got Married* — but again they gave him the opportunity to be "out there" with his acting. Portraying a computer-hacking star-nosed mole is definitely something he'd never done before.

So while Cage could have stayed on his oddball-weirdo trajectory and, presumably, maintained a cult following somewhat like his colleague (and former high-school buddy) Crispin Glover, instead he is constantly weaving in new directions. "When I started acting, I was much more of an anarchist," said Cage in a 1998 interview with the *Globe and Mail*. "I was only interested in doing movies like *Wild at Heart* and *Vampire's Kiss*, more rebellious, kind of punk-rock, alternative expressions. I became aware that I was about to intense or weird myself right out of the business. I had to balance."

Never wanting to get into a rut or do too much of the same thing, every few years (or, in some cases, every few movies) he makes a left turn and heads into new territory. After making darker films like *Wild at Heart* (1990) and *Zandalee* (1991) — a New Orleans drama where Cage plays a moody artist who has an affair with his friend's wife with deadly consequences — Cage was inspired to move into more lighthearted fare by his grandmother and Jim Morrison.

In a *New York Times* interview, Cage said he was intrigued by Jim Morrison's desire to make a song that "conveyed pure happiness." That, mixed with his maternal grandmother's desire to see her grandson make some happier movies that would make her laugh, led him in the early '90s to what he calls his Sunshine Trilogy: *Honeymoon in Vegas*, *Guarding Tess*, and *It Could Happen to You*. In *Honeymoon*, Cage figured out how to bring his weirdo character acting skills into a leading man role. Playing opposite Sarah Jessica Parker's grade school teacher, Betsy, Cage's Jack is a somewhat anxiety-ridden nice guy who is torn between loving his girlfriend and a promise he made to his dying mother (Anne Bancroft) that he would never wed. As Jack gets sucked deeper and deeper into the weird web that James Caan's Tommy Korman has woven, his frustration comes out in little Cagey bursts. The hilarious and perfect facial expressions he worked out in *Raising Arizona* come back a little smaller here, lending humor and spirit to the character. Take the first scene when his mother dies, and his eyes bug out and his mouth opens wider than seems humanly possible, or the disbelief and nausea that heave from his body when he loses $65,000 to Korman. Beyond pleasing his grandmother, taking a role like Jack in *Honeymoon in Vegas* was a good move for Cage. It's one of the first instances of Cage overlapping his character actor skills with a leading man role.

Honeymoon also gave him a taste of the joy that comes with sharing a comedy with an audience. So he made more. Maybe looking at Cage's gawky teen punk in *Valley Girl* and his operatic suicidal romantic in *Moonstruck* prepared us for his turn as a romantic lead, but it was still a departure when the man who had mostly been playing weirdoes was suddenly the moral hero. (*Valley Girl*'s Randy wasn't the usual teen movie heartthrob either. He was the rebellious underdog we rooted for, but he wasn't the hunk we're used to being told to love. He was lanky, bushy eyebrowed, crooked toothed, and had weirdly shaped body hair.[17]) We were used to seeing him as oddballs and rebels, not a straight-laced secret service agent (*Guarding Tess*) or a cop with a heart of gold (*It Could Happen to You*).

At the end of the Sunshine Trilogy, Cage did another light comedy: 1994's *Trapped in Paradise*, co-starring Dana Carvey and Jon Lovitz as Cage's criminal brothers. The film sees Cage as the straight man to Carvey and Lovitz's bumbling criminal partnership as the three try to rob a bank on Christmas Eve. For Cage, this was too much of the same. Once filming was finished, he decided he was done making comedies in that vein for a while. The next role he jumped on was Little Junior Brown in *Kiss of Death* (1995).

This was an odd role for Cage for a number of reasons, not the least of which was because he was only a supporting character in the film. By 1995, Cage had become an above-the-title name and, at the very least, shared the marquee with another actor. But he chose to play this significantly smaller part to David Caruso's leading man because it was the opposite of all the sweet characters he had been playing, and he found Little Junior Brown interesting. "To me it was like, finally, I was going to be able to get the stink off me of that last

---

17 Even though Cage was only 19 at the time the movie was filmed, he was asked to trim his chest hair because the heavy growth made him look older, and he came back with it shaved into a triangle.

experience," said Cage in a *Rolling Stone* interview that year, referring to *Trapped in Paradise*. "To blow out of this state of schmaltz that I can't stand."

There's no schmaltz on Junior Brown. He's a thick-necked thug who can toss a man through the air or bench press a woman (both things he actually does in the film). It's easy to see why Cage was attracted to Little Junior. He has the requisite number of quirks to make him an attractive challenge for Cage, who would have to make a man who brutally beats people to a pulp into a compelling bad guy. He punches Michael Rapaport to death while wearing a rain poncho (but says "ow" afterward as he looks at his fist covered in blood); he wears all white and likes to keep everything clean, including his boom box, which he wipes down meticulously after Rapaport's blood gets splattered on it; he can only eat with plastic cutlery because he can't stand the taste of metal in his mouth; and when his father dies, he mourns by jumping up and down in a strip club, crying. His major obstacle as a mob man under pressure is his asthma. He's equal parts quirky and menacing, and the portrayal caused Ebert to call Little Junior "the weirdest villain since Dennis Hopper slithered into *Blue Velvet*."

This character, another shift in his constantly moving career, triggered an article in *Sight and Sound* devoted to pondering what Nic Cage was up to. "Is Nicolas Cage the greatest American actor?" the first sentence of the article wondered. Comparing Cage to Robert De Niro, James Dean, and Marlon Brando, the author tentatively agreed with Pauline Kael, who often picked Cage out for doing great things in mediocre movies; the article describes Cage as an authentic, constantly changing presence no matter the film: "He shifts gears from unlikely romantic ideal to unspeakable geek, often in the very same movie." Within movies and between movies, you never know which Nic Cage to expect.

In the interest of constant change, when he was offered the Jeff Daniels role in *Dumb and Dumber*, he turned it down for the low-paying independent film *Leaving Las Vegas*. Judging by Cage's past method of choosing work, he made this decision because he needed something fresh, and *Dumb and Dumber* may have been too close to the goofy comedies he'd just come out of. In hindsight, the lure of *Vegas*'s Ben Sanderson seems obvious — it is one of his most lauded (and definitely most awarded) roles, there's relative freedom and depth to be found in playing a man who is letting go of everything to die, and if Cage enjoys going outside the box, playing a drunk is definitely one of the places that makes allowances for that. However, taking on such a dark role in such a small movie was also a risk. For someone who was worried about being typecast as the "eccentric, avant-garde actor" and weirding himself out of the business, this was a dangerous place to go just after settling in as a mainstream leading man.

But it worked. Aside from the acclaim he received because of it, *Leaving Las Vegas* was the right choice for Cage because he proved that he could pull off serious, heartbreaking realism. In one scene, Ben Sanderson returns to Sera's apartment after spending the morning at a bar getting head-butted by a guy in a leather vest. Looking at his face covered in blood, Sera, played by Elisabeth Shue, asks him how he's feeling. Cage added his own response, singing, "Like the Kling Klang King of the Rim Ram Room." The addition of this line took director Mike Figgis off guard, and he criticized Cage on set for improvising. But Cage wasn't improvising on the spot. He had thought out that bit very carefully before he tried it on set, and it made it into the final cut of the film. "He's still very sensitive about the perception that he's wacky, because his performance isn't that," said Figgis in an *Entertainment Weekly* interview. "It's all hard work. Nothing in it is arbitrary."

Nothing is. He saw *City of Angels* (1998) as a chance to do a more introverted performance, trying his best to approximate what it would be like to be an entity that was not human and that worked purely in goodness. He did *Adaptation* because he admired Jeremy Irons's take on twins in David Cronenberg's *Dead Ringers* and wanted to give it his own spin.[18] From 2007 until at least 2010, Cage's interests diverted to the supernatural, and he chose films like *Knowing*,[19] *Next*, *Ghost Rider*, and *The Sorcerer's Apprentice* because he felt there were infinite possibilities for what he could do with characters in movies where otherworldly things were happening.

One key point on Cage's Advance Genius meter is *Deadfall*, a neo-noir directed by Cage's brother Christopher Coppola

---

18 He chose to play Donald and Charlie in *Adaptation* over the Green Goblin in *Spiderman* — something we can point to as a clear good decision.

19 *Knowing* (2009) did not review well, but Roger Ebert enthusiastically came to its defense, calling it one of the best science fiction films he'd ever seen. What Ebert liked best about *Knowing* was that it brought up questions about whether the universe is deterministic or random: an interesting parallel debate given what I'm arguing about Cage's choices.

about a constantly overlapping series of cons and double crosses within a family of scammers. In it, Cage plays Eddie, lackey to James Coburn's Lou, who is trying to stop Lou's nephew (Michael Biehn) from nosing in on the family business. Cage did *Deadfall* because his brother was directing and, like his tiny role in *Never on Tuesday* — where Cage is onscreen for all of 30 seconds, wearing a fake nose that he specifically requested, using a squeezed, breathy voice, and laughing hysterically — his bit part gave him the freedom to go more "out there" than he ever had before. As a rage-filled cokehead, the opportunities for lunacy are infinite, and Cage goes further than ever. Often compared to Dennis Hopper's Frank Booth from *Blue Velvet*, Cage's Eddie speaks as though he has his jaw wired shut and shouts expletives as if he's singing. Getting to put his Western Kabuki style into practice, a pencil-mustached Cage flails his body as much as possible, fighting with a coat hanger and having a furious tantrum on a bed. In a featurette for the film, Nic says he was not trying to bring any logic to his villainous character; instead he just wanted to do whatever came naturally without editing himself. Though this seems classically Cagey, when you keep in mind that his performances are generally carefully planned, this too is a bold experiment, and one that worked: Cage's intense performance is the only element of the largely forgettable film that is still talked about.

If we take Thelonius Monk's definition of a genius as "the one most like himself," Cage's genius comes from his willingness to do whatever works for him despite what's expected. His choices are hard to reconcile because each movie he makes is for a different audience. It's hard to hang on to a hardcore fan-base when you go from *Face/Off* to *City of Angels* to *Bringing Out the Dead.* And then who's left to defend your work when they don't like (or don't understand) two out of every three movies you make? The fans who love him for *Vampire's Kiss*, *Wild at Heart*, and *Bad Lieutenant* are not necessarily the same ones who love him for *Gone in 60 Seconds*, *Ghost Rider*, and *Kick-Ass.* And this split leads to all the groups questioning his decision-making when the next film he makes is not in the realm of what they want or expect.

At 2014's South by Southwest festival, in answer to a question about how he chooses his roles, Cage said, "Always stay a student, never be a maestro."

Nicolas Cage sees himself as a student of film. He wants to feel uncomfortable, so he can learn from the experience. His desire to learn is the main influence on his choice of films. He looks for something that will challenge him by making him try something he hasn't tried before. He looks for opportunities to work in other countries,[20] with directors from whom he can gain new inspiration. While other actors with his tenure may have made the transition from student to teacher long ago, he looks for films where he can work with new actors, so he can learn from younger generations who may be coming up with a different approach to their craft.[21] In a *HitFix* interview, he

---

20 As long as the work doesn't keep him away from his family for too long. He turned down the role of Aragorn in Peter Jackson's *Lord of the Rings* trilogy because filming in New Zealand would take him too far away from his family.

21 The learning is reciprocal. Young actors such as Jay Baruchel and Tye Sheridan have gushed about Cage-as-teacher in interviews.

likens his approach to Miles Davis, who worked with younger musicians to keep his feet in what was happening at the time, so as not to get stale. Cage feels that's what he's doing with acting. His acting is akin to jazz. "It's important not to get too comfortable with whatever it is you're doing," he said, "and it's also important not to play only songs that you love."

4

The Man, the Myth, the Meme

"Your problem is you're much too beautiful for this kind of
work. Me? I'm everyman."
— Nicolas Cage in *Honeymoon in Vegas*

In grade four, young Nicolas was being bullied at school. So
he created a "cousin" character, a cross between James Dean
and Clint Eastwood: he wore sunglasses and cowboy boots,
had his hair slicked back, and chewed gum with attitude, or so
Cage described him in a 1995 *Rolling Stone* profile. Pretending
to be this character he called "Roy Richards," Cage threat-
ened the bully with an ass kicking if he bothered young Nicky
again. The performance worked. One could argue that this
smudging of the line between character and reality continues

today: we can't separate Cage from the characters he plays, or perhaps a bizarre composite of all his most Cagey roles.

This is only fueled by the beyond-belief stories about him offscreen. If we hear he was spotted at McDonald's, that's the real shocker, not that the dinosaur bones he owns might be illegal, or that he was hanging out at a haunted house with Carrot Top and Vince Neil — wearing matching orange sport coats, no less — before going to a Coolio concert. As critic Nathan Rabin put it in his Year of Flops review of *Drive Angry* on the *A.V. Club*: "Is it Cage that has a lucky crack pipe and hates to see dead souls dance, or his character in *Bad Lieutenant: Port of Call New Orleans*? Did the Elvis-worshipping ex-con Cage played in *Wild at Heart* marry the King's daughter, or does that distinction belong to Elvis acolyte Cage himself?"

Rabin continues, "We need Cage to be crazy in real life, or else the lunacy of his performances would feel inauthentic." We're still looking for a sort of realism: Cage constantly playing a version of his eccentric self.

To be fair, the desire to believe Cage is *really* larger than life has been, at times, helped along by Cage himself. In 1992 he somersaulted onto the stage of the British chat show *Wogan*, proceeded to throw what looked like money into the audience, and finished with a high kick. Mid-interview, he ripped off his shirt and gave it to host Terry Wogan then punched at the audience. He's widely quoted as having once said, "I am not a demon. I am a lizard, a shark, a heat-seeking panther. I want to be Bob Denver on acid playing the accordion." It's one of the most popular quotes you'll find associated with Nicolas Cage, but an original source for it is harder to find. Perhaps he said it, perhaps he didn't — either way, it has become the definition of Cage for many.

In his March 2014 *Grantland* article about SXSW, Alex Pappademas covers Nicolas Cage's appearance at the screening of *Joe*. He describes a moment when, during his appearance, Cage inexplicably started making strange faces and standing in weird positions. This, Pappademas thought, was exactly what he expected from a weirdo like Cage.

But then he realized that Cage wasn't pondering the ceiling or trying to figure out where he was; he was just posing for the many photographs that the audience was snapping during the talk. "He is embracing the unnaturalness of a wholly unnatural situation by becoming an unnatural being, projecting an idea of himself that makes no sense in person but will come to life when his image is broadcast and tweeted and Instagrammed around the world," writes Pappademas. As a famous actor, he constantly exists in unnatural situations. It might be playing a guy who thinks he's a vampire or a man who is turning into a flaming skull, or playing himself in the midst of his stardom. Red carpet performances are exaggeration to the point of satire. Cage is acknowledging Hollywood celebrity for what it is: a performance that has as much to do with reality as "reality TV." Which is perhaps a surprisingly sane thing to do.

But the myth also takes on a life of its own. A photo of a man from the civil war era started circulating in 2011 as "proof" that Nicolas Cage is a vampire. The photo bears a striking resemblance to Cage (but also, oddly, to a young

Martin Short as Ed Grimley) and is repeatedly posted along-side photos of present-day Cage.[22]

Cage has been so many people, in so many roles, he is a vessel that can contain almost anything we pour into it: as long as that thing is a bit Cagey. Nothing combines his conceptual integrity with his physical malleability as much as the explosion of Nicolas Cage memes.

For the uninitiated (or those who just don't spend any time online), a meme is an idea or behavior that spreads from person to person through some form of communication. While any shared image or unit of culture is a meme, in the case of an internet meme, it's typically an image or catchphrase that moves across the internet and transforms as each person adds their own version to the conversation. Be it a surprised-looking cat, the disappointed face of an Olympic gymnast, or Sean Bean in *Lord of the Rings* saying "One does not simply speak in a normal voice to their pet,"[23] to be the most successful of memes, an image must be relatable and flexible.

If there's one thing people who love him and hate him both seem to enjoy, it's Cage-as-internet-meme. One of the most popular Nicolas Cage meme-based websites so far has been *Nic Cage as Everyone*, a website that takes advantage of the flexibility of Cage's face by putting it on people, animals, cartoon characters, objects, and other memes. Similar sites

---

22 Cage has been asked about the theory and he says he doesn't buy it. His defense: there are photos of him, and since vampires don't show up in photographs, he thinks he's in the clear. (Also he can see himself in the mirror and says he doesn't drink blood.)

23 It's a play on his line from *Lord of the Rings*: "One does not simply walk into Mordor." Bean really rivals Cage for most memed actor.

have popped up, such as a "Nicolas Cage's Face on Things" Facebook group. I asked the makers of Nicolas Cage's Face on Things what the allure of Cage was for this medium. They simply saw the humor in "his [facial] expressions and mannerisms" and in the juxtaposition they created when put into opposing serious or sweet contexts. But I think the reason his face works on all the characters from *Lord of the Rings* and on all the Sailor Scouts is because of his proven ability to take on any genre and play any role. Further, Nic Cage isn't known for blending into the wallpaper: sticking out, playing against form and expectation, is what he's made a career out of.

People have also taken up something they call "Caging": pasting photos of Nicolas Cage all over someone's home or office (he's under toilet lids, on the back of airplane seats, in ice cube trays). Someone turned their back windshield wiper into an image of Nicolas Cage waving. Cage in unexpected places is funny, of course, but again, it makes a kind of sense. We never know where he'll pop up next in the filmscape. Predictability? Not his thing.

Jesse Wente, head of film programmes at the Toronto International Film Festival's Bell Lightbox cinema and programmer of 2012's Bangkok Dangerous: The Cinema of Nicolas Cage, tells me, "The fact that he seems to live a larger-than-life existence offscreen . . . it lends itself to that sort of engagement." Part of the intrigue of memes is to create a stereotype and roll with it until it either gets out of control or dies. The Cagey stereotype is mania. One of the most popular supercuts featuring Cage is a collection called "Nicolas

Cage Losing His Shit," which features over four minutes of Cage moaning, yelling, laughing, gagging, throwing things, punching women, and screaming "fuuuuuck" for a full five seconds. One of the first memes of Cage revolved around a still of his face from *Vampire's Kiss*. It's the face he makes when he's telling his secretary that he wouldn't give anyone else other than her the terrible job of sifting through old contracts. In the audio commentary for *Vampire's Kiss*, Cage said he was experimenting in that scene to see how wide he could get his eyes. They are huge, and his nostrils are flared. A line drawing of that facial expression accompanied by the words "You Don't Say?" started rounding the internet in 2011 to point out really obvious statements. Anytime someone spotted an unnecessary clarification — like a bag of carrots that listed "carrots" as the sole ingredient or a body of water accompanied by a sign that reads "road closed due to flooding" — they could let that bug-eyed face do the talking.

Cage's face was the inspiration for artist Brandon Bird, creator of works featuring Nicolas Cage, *Law and Order*, and Christopher Walken. His Nicolas Cage pieces started with an oil painting called *Uncanny Valley*, which features Cage as a snow monkey.

"It began with a friend mentioning how much he looked like a snow monkey," said Bird via email from California, "and things snowballed from there." He then made the Nicolas Cage Adventure Set (a collection of colorforms that allow users to put various iterations of Nicolas Cage and props on settings in outer space, a cave, and a tropical island). The popularity of the adventure set alone is further proof that Cage's experiment is working. Cage has managed to position himself in so many different settings across his career that we want to put him in rocket boots holding a keytar next to a basket of kittens. He's made anything make sense with his image.

Bird isn't the only artist using Cage as their muse. In 2013, Buzzfeed staffer Jen Lewis illustrated Nicolas Cage's face on all your favorite Disney princesses,[24] and in early 2014, a California DJ named Ezra Croft turned Cage's face into a San Francisco gallery show when he put out a call for artists to submit work inspired by the actor. In April of that year he held a packed event called the Nicolas Cage Art Show featuring hundreds of pieces, most of which played with Cage's face in various forms.

"To me, Nicolas Cage represents the potential in all of us," Croft told the *Huffington Post*. "The potential to make the less than perfect decisions, but to do so with intensity and grandeur that others aren't willing to have. Like Cage, you have to get out there and make things happen, whether or not people love it or hate it!"

The show featured works akin to the memes — a painting of Sailor Moon with Cage's face, his face on a unicorn, a holy portrait of St. Nicolas of Cage — but also original works that were inspired by Cage — one portrait in particular showed the actor's versatility by putting three versions of him (from *Lord of War*, *Con Air*, and *Raising Arizona*) together as a family. But by the time Croft ran a similar show in L.A. in July of the same

---

24 This was the meme people forwarded to me the most that year.

year, critics were declaring the Cage meme dead. (But if we've learned anything, it's that critics can't control Cage.)

A *Vice* magazine article claimed the show and its meme-worthy artworks had successfully flogged the joke of the Cage meme to death by simply recreating images of his face on things without saying anything new. "I can't help but think that an opportunity was missed. A lot of these works — which were beautifully done by talented people — could have turned fan art into something more. Not to be a total art snob, but there's something to say about the recreation of digital art as fine art, about pop culture in relation to intellectual art. There's something to say about celebrity and the loss of personhood when one attains such a level of fame."

Is his face on a killer whale not talking about his loss of personhood? While *Vice* may think the memes aren't saying anything except "Hey, look at Nicolas Cage if he was a Pokémon, ha ha," the act of putting his face on everything is talking, however inadvertently, about celebrity culture. Bringing Cage outside of his movies and into other forms of media shows that Cage's relevance to us goes beyond his own creations. It has taken on a life of its own. His diversity as an actor and the longevity of his career speak directly to the durability of his meme. We won't be saying goodbye to Cage-as-meme any time soon.[25]

As we experience entertainment in more fragmented ways, a successful celebrity needs to hit us on as many levels as possible.

---

25 One does not simply stop making Nicolas Cage memes.

This is something Cage figured out really early on[26] by targeting work in all genres. But even more contemporary celebs, such as Drake, are embracing their potential to be memes and making it work for them. They realize they can use them for marketing, to expose their faces and their brand to more eyeballs.

There is some interview evidence that Cage is rolling with his memedom, but his ultimate endorsement came in 2014, when a photo of him hanging out with Andrew Dice Clay at a Guns N' Roses concert went viral, not because of the company he was keeping but because he was wearing a shirt with his own face on it.[27] It was the "You Don't Say" meme, and the act of wearing it (along with the few moments in interviews when he's said that he doesn't understand the meme, but he's rolling with it) was an embrace — or at least an acceptance — of his face as meme.

He may be accepting his morphed form of celebrity online, but he doesn't want it to overwhelm the work he's doing onscreen. In his public talk with *Joe* director David Gordon Green at SXSW, Cage lamented the direction celebrity is taking and the fact that even film critics are letting the actors' outside lives be the subject of reviews. "What the hell does Lindsay Lohan's personal life have to do with her performance in *The Canyons*? It should always be about the work itself," he said. He doesn't want to see a time when people only know him as the "You Don't Say" face and not as an actor.

---

26 ADVANCED GENIUS.

27 In truth, the rest of his outfit was more interesting than the shirt. He was wearing a cowboy hat, aviators, chaps, numerous necklaces and bracelets, and was holding a cane.

Despite the fact that many of these memes (and critics) are constantly picking apart his actions to make fun of him, even the ones that are aiming to be critical of his acting ability are simultaneously pointing out exactly why he's a great actor. If people think he must be exactly like the characters he plays in real life — if Cage embodies these roles so completely that the audience truly believes he must be these characters — then he has done his job. We believe him. We believe him so hard we can't imagine that he's even acting. He just *is* all of his characters. Or so he has us convinced.

As with his seemingly erratic film choices and his off-the-wall performances, all of this may just be disguising his genius. We may be taking part in a narrative of Cage's own making. Bird, for all his snow monkey art, thinks the actor no fool: "My impression is that he is a lot smarter than he is given credit for, and that he's definitely in on the joke . . . but the joke is one he's telling and it's sailing over everyone's heads." It's Nic Cage's meme, we're just sharing it.

5

The Cage Experiment

"There are often lists of the great living male movie stars: De Niro, Nicholson and Pacino, usually. How often do you see the name of Nicolas Cage? He should always be up there."
— Roger Ebert

Cage understands how we see him. In a 2014 "What I've Learnt" feature in the London *Times Magazine*, Nicolas Cage ran through the many lessons he has learned through over 30 years of acting:

I'm proud of the chances I've taken. They haven't all worked, but I had a concept and I've pushed for it. It's probably annoyed a lot of critics and a lot of people who didn't get in step with it, but I'm proud I did it. Tolstoy said something to the effect of, it doesn't matter whether the response you get is love or hatred, because you've created an effect. What's not worthwhile is when it sits there and people forget about it. But whether people love it or hate it, at least you've done something. That gives me some solace.

And Cage is anything but forgettable. He may not be able to change the public's idea of "good" film acting overnight, but he's hacking away at it. If art is fundamentally about generating a reaction, then Cage has been more successful than most actors. And his career, like his life, is his ultimate work-in-progress. It's performance mixed with performance art, and with every film we see, every meme we share, we're a part of it.

"To me, Nicolas Cage is a guy that is on a film-to-film, year-to-year basis, involved in that sort of constant rethinking about what this guy is," said Jesse Wente. "Because every time critics want to write him off as a guy doing paycheck movies and bizarre performance choices, he does *Joe* and suddenly you're like, 'Well, that's fascinating and now I have to reset again.'"

Yet we don't have to reset if we view the films as a continuous body of work. He's played yuppies, scumbags, honorable rogues, heroes, villains, a gangster, a lovelorn punk, a pair of screenwriters, a greasy weapons dealer, at least a dozen cops and ex-cons, an angel, a mechanic, a pimp, a scientist, a scholar, a star-nosed mole, a con man, a caveman, and a weatherman. And with each one, he's put in the same amount of dedication.

It's this dedication that we need. With an abundance of cynicism in our media — the most popular cultural writing favors snark over sincerity — Cage is a reminder that it's okay to care, even if it makes you look ridiculous. Though success is a vital part of the American mythos, Cage has never been afraid to look like a failure. He doesn't want to be cool, he wants to be creative. He chooses to make himself uncomfortable with each new role to ensure he's always learning. He defies definition on purpose, so he is never typecast, never static.

During the Pivot questionnaire portion of *Inside the Actors Studio* — the part where host James Lipton asks actors about their favorite swear words and turn-ons — Nicolas Cage had the most revealing answers. If he ever meets God at the "pearly gates" he hope his greeting would be "bless you for trying." And his least favorite word: "stop." No matter how impossible it is to predict what Cage is going to do next, there's one thing we can predict with some surety: he will not stop.

*Sources

"Nicolas Cage is a metaphor for God, or for society, or for the self, or something . . ." Quotation from: Lewis, Jennifer. "The Best of 'Dan Harmon with a Microphone' at Communicon." *Flavorwire*. February 10, 2013.

"Right smack in the centre of a contradiction — that's the place to be. That's where the energy is, that's where the heat is" Bono. *Zoo Radio*. BBC Radio 1. January 1, 1993.

"I thought [Cage] was interesting as it had two sides, the popcorn side and the more thoughtful side . . ." Aftab, Kaleem.

"Nicolas Cage Interview: Still Wild at Heart." *The Independent*. July 25, 2014.

Audio commentary from Mike Werb and John Woo. *Face/Off*. Dir. John Woo. 1997. Paramount, 2008. DVD.

"Liberace of crime" Daly, Steve. "Face to Face." *Entertainment Weekly*. June 20, 1997. 20–24.

"Even at the first reading he had the two characters beautifully delineated . . ." Hobson, Louis B. "Two for the Show." *The Sunday Sun*. December 1, 2002. 30.

Baron, Cynthia. "Performances in Adaptation: Analyzing Human Movement in Motion Pictures." *Cineast* 31.4 (2006). 48–55.

"Fear of trying something new, something that wasn't just more of the same" "An Interview with Jon Schnepp, the Man Behind 'The Death of Superman Lives: What Happened?'" *Everything Action*. March 9, 2013.

"Unless you're a total cynical dick, you have to embrace the fact that Nicolas Cage is a pretty good actor" Lewis, Jennifer. "The Best of 'Dan Harmon with a Microphone' at Communicon."

Brockes, Emma. "Nicolas Cage: 'People think I'm not in on the joke.'" *The Guardian*. July 20, 2013.

Silvia, Paul J. "Looking Past Pleasure: Anger, Confusion, Disgust, Pride, Surprise, and Other Unusual Aesthetic Emotions." *Psychology of Aesthetics, Creativity and the Arts* 3.1 (2009). 48–51.

"Naturalism is a style that can be really effective, but it can be really boring" Winer-Bernheimer, Linda. "A Castle with a Different Cage: He's 30, a Parent, and Taking a Rest from 'Twisted Characters.'" *Los Angeles Times*. July 25, 1994.

The inspiration Cage used for Smokey in *Rumble Fish* from: Cage, Nicolas. *On Location in Tulsa: The Making of Rumble Fish*. *Rumble Fish*. Dir. Frances Ford Coppola, 1983. Universal, 2005. DVD.

"Emotional vomit" and "I wanted to put back into acting a more surreal . . ." Rowland, Mark. "The Beasts Within . . . Nicolas Cage." *American Film* 15.9 (1990). 22–29.

"In dreams, oftentimes, things are weird and distorted . . ." Gelmis, Joseph. "Cage Steps Out from a Curtain of Privacy." *Newsday*. October 11, 1986.

"I think David Lynch's movies are more real than Spielberg's . . ." Rowland, Mark. "The Beasts within . . . Nicolas Cage."

"If it wasn't for her, I don't think I would have been able to act . . ." Schruers, Fred. "Dangerous, Dedicated and Wild at

Heart: Nicolas Cage Is a Hollywood Samurai." *Rolling Stone*. November 16, 1995. 93–121.

Denby, David. "Peggy Sue Got Married." *New York Magazine*. October 20, 1986: 90–92.

Kirkland, Bruce. "Peggy Sue Got Married." *Toronto Sun*. October 10, 1986.

Ansen, David. "Peggy Sue Got Married." *Newsweek*. October 6, 1986.

Kael, Pauline. "Peggy Sue Got Married." *New Yorker*. October 20, 1986.

"When I see retrospectives and that character comes on . . ." Schruers, Fred. "The Passion of Nicolas Cage." *Rolling Stone*. November 11, 1999.

"The rumor around town was . . ." Audio commentary from Norman Jewison and Cher. *Moonstruck*. Dir. Norman Jewison, 1987. Sony, 2006. DVD.

"I'm not the first one to do it . . ." "Nicolas Cage: 'Sometimes it's good to be hated.'" *The Talks*. August 13, 2014.

"to use my voice in almost a heavy-metal . . ." Miller, Julie.

"Nicolas Cage on *Joe*, the Calming Effect of Venomous Snakes, and Why He's Been So 'Over-the-Top' in Movies Lately." *Vanity Fair*. September 11, 2013.

"onyx or tourmaline or something . . ." "Exclusive: Nicolas Cage Reveals 'Nouveau Shamanic.'" *ITN Entertainment*. February 13, 2012.

"He's the only actor since Marlon Brando . . ." Hawke, Ethan. "I Am Ethan Hawke — AMAA." Reddit. June 5, 2013.

"Silent film is another country . . ." Denby, David. "The Artists." *New Yorker*. February 27, 2012.

Zucker, Carole. "The Concept of 'Excess' In Film Acting: Notes Toward an Understanding of Non-Naturalistic Performance." *Post Script* 12.2 (1993). 54–62.

"almost like silent film, like Lon Chaney . . ." Ebert, Roger. "'Bringing Out' Scorsese." *Chicago Sun-Times*. October 21, 1999.

"He does some of the way-out stuff . . ." Kael, Pauline. "Vampire's Kiss." *New Yorker*. June 12, 1989.

"Every one of those moves was thought out . . ." Audio commentary from Nicolas Cage and Robert Bierman. *Vampire's Kiss*. Dir. Robert Bierman, 1989. MGM, 2002. DVD.

"Continental bullshit accent . . ." Fitch, J. "Vampire's Kiss." *American Film* 14.8 (1989). 67–68.

"Look at me! I'm acting!" James, Caryn. "Vampire's Kiss (1989)." *New York Times*. June 2, 1989.

"No one can glance sideways better . . ." Ebert, Roger. "Seeking Justice." Ebert.com. March 14, 2012.

"When I act, I hear the dialogue . . ." "Nicolas Cage: a fan of Chinese cinema." *CCTV News*. Online video clip. YouTube. October 21, 2013.

"Outrageously unbridled performance . . ." Rosenbaum, Jonathan. "Vampire's Kiss." *Chicago Reader*. June 1, 1989.

"This film requires [Cage] to start at . . ." Tobias, Scott. "Vampire's Kiss features one of Nicolas Cage's best, most out-of-control performances." *A.V. Club*. May 24, 2012.

"The day will come when naturalism will die . . ." Audio Commentary from Nicolas Cage and Robert Bierman. *Vampire's Kiss*.

"If you can get very outside the box . . ." "Ghost Rider — Spirit of Vengeance: Nicolas Cage interview." IndieLondon.co.uk. 2011.

"they are both made restless by caution . . ." Ebert, Roger. "Bad Lieutenant: Port of Call, New Orleans" Ebert.com. November 18, 2009.

"There's a lot of things that make Nic unique . . ." Rowland, Mark. "The Beasts Within . . . Nicolas Cage."

"Mr. Cage, once a champion over-the-top actor . . ." James, Caryn. "Red Rock West: The New Boy in Town Ruled By Coincidence." *New York Times*. April 8, 1994.

"You look at his face . . ." Schruers, Fred. "The Passion of Nicolas Cage."

"more than a rescue . . ." Mondello, Bob. "Big Names, High Production Values . . . And These Are Indie Flicks?" NPR. April 11, 2014.

"some of his best actorly qualities . . ." Schager, Nick. "Nicolas Cage Doesn't Need a McConaissance." *Vulture*. April 11, 2014.

"He always seems so earnest . . ." Ebert, Roger. "Adaptation." *Chicago Sun-Times*. December 20, 2002.

"What's the point in just getting good reviews?" "The Total Film Interview — Nicolas Cage." *Games Radar*. November 9, 2005.

"I can't get used up . . ." Brockes, Emma. "Nicolas Cage: 'People think I'm not in on the joke.'"

"early innovation that is not immediately appreciated" and "a great artist is great because" Hartley, Jason. *The Advanced Genius Theory*. Scribner: New York. 2010.

"be as naked as I can be as a film presence . . ." Brockes, Emma. "Nicolas Cage: 'People think I'm not in on the joke.'"

"big-budget, action pictures . . ." Siskel, Gene. "Wisecracking Nicolas Cage Saves Hyperactive Thriller 'The Rock.'" *Chicago Tribune*. June 7, 1996.

"I want new experiences . . ." "Nicolas Cage: A Fan of Chinese Cinema." *CCTV News*.

"*The Rock* really taught me a lot . . ." Audio commentary from Nicolas Cage. *The Rock*. Dir. Michael Bay, 1996. The Criterion Collection, 2001. DVD.

"The manner is a combination of Elvis . . ." Thompson, Bob. "A Cagey Situtation." *Sunday Sun*. June 1, 1997.

"When I started acting, I was much more of an anarchist . . ." Strauss, Bob. "Nicolas Cage Best on a Balancing Act." *Globe and Mail*. August 10, 1998.

"conveyed pure happiness . . ." Pall, Ellen. "Nicolas Cage: The Sunshine Man." *New York Times*. July 24, 1994.

"To me it was like, finally . . ." Schruers, Fred. "Dangerous, Dedicated and Wild at Heart: Nicolas Cage is a Hollywood Samurai."

"the weirdest villain since Dennis Hopper . . ." Ebert, Roger. "Kiss of Death." *Chicago Sun-Times*. April 21, 1995.

"Is Nicolas Cage the greatest American actor?" Dargis, Manohla. "Method and Madness." *Sight and Sound* 5.6 (June 1995). 6–8.

"He's still very sensitive . . ." Daly, Steve. "High Spirits." *Entertainment Weekly*. March 15, 1996.

"Always stay a student . . ." Smith, Nigel M. "Here Are the Best Things Nicolas Cage Said During His Career-Spanning SXSW Talk." *Indie Wire*. March 11, 2014.

"It's important not to get too comfortable . . ." "Epic Nicolas Cage Interview Discussing Sorcerer's Apprentice, Kick-Ass and Even The Wicker Man." *HitFix*. YouTube. April 8, 2010.

"Roy Richards" Schruers, Fred. "Dangerous, Dedicated and Wild at Heart: Nicolas Cage is a Hollywood Samurai."

"Is it Cage that has a lucky crack pipe . . ." Rabin, Nathan. "Written Entirely in 3D Case File #184: Drive Angry 3D." *A.V. Club*. March 16, 2011.

"He is embracing the unnaturalness . . ." Pappademas, Alex. "SXSW Notebook." *Grantland*. March 13, 2014.

"his [facial] expressions and mannerisms . . ." Facebook message from Nicolas Cage's Face on Things. March 28, 2013.

All Jesse Wente quotations from personal interview. September 24, 2014.

All Brandon Bird quotations from email interview. September 8, 2014.

"To me, Nicolas Cage represents . . ." Frank, Priscilla. "We're Not Ready for the Intensity of a Nicolas Cage Art Show." *Huffington Post*. March 17, 2014.

"I can't help but think . . ." Stevenson, Alison. "The Nicolas Cage Art Show Finally Killed the Nicolas Cage Meme." *Vice*. July 23, 2014.

"What the hell does Lindsay Lohan's personal life . . ." Bacardi, Francesca. "Nicolas Cage at SXSW: 'It Sucks to Be Famous Right Now.'" *Variety*. March 10, 2014.

"There are often lists . . ." Ebert, Roger. "Adaptation."

"I'm proud of the chances I've taken . . ." Machell, Ben. "What I've Learnt: Nicolas Cage." *The Times Magazine*. September 20, 2014.

"Inside the Actor's Studio with Nicolas Cage." *Inside the Actor's Studio*. YouTube. February 7, 2015.

Acknowledgments

I'd like to thank the following people for their support through the creation of this book:

Matthew Daley for buying me almost all of Nicolas Cage's films, watching so many movies with me, listening to me talk about Cage endlessly, and all the love and support you've given me and my Cage obsession.

Jesse Wente for programing the Nicolas Cage retrospective at the TIFF Bell Lightbox cinema and amping up my Cage obsession.

Jen Knoch, Crissy Calhoun, and ECW for turning my obsession into a job and for helping me to shape my complicated thoughts about Cage (and reminding me to say more than just CAGE IS THE BEST over and over).

Jenna Illies for asking people to read this book.

The Nicolas Cage Film Festival club for sharing in (or at least tolerating) my obsession for over three years.

Richard Rosenbaum for all your book-pitching & book-writing advice.

Aaron Manczyk and Queen Video for all the Cage rentals and chats.

Vakis Boutsalis for being my best cheerleader (and PR man).

Kelly Boutsalis, Christine Clarke, and Andrea Nene for starting our first film festival/debate club and giving me the tools to write this thing.

Rachel Beattie and Michelle Lovegrove Thomson at the TIFF Film Reference Library for all your research help and enthusiasm for Cage studies.

My parents for treating this book like their grandchild.

The Ontario Arts Council for their support through the Writers' Reserve program.

Alison Lang for being so great, Hal Niedzviecki for being a mentor and a friend, and everyone at *Broken Pencil* magazine for their constant awesomeness.

Lindsay Gibb is a librarian and journalist with a specific interest in zines, film, and comics. She co-programs the Toronto Comic Arts Festival's Librarian and Educator Day, and her writing has appeared in *Shameless*, *This Magazine*, and *Playback*. She was the editor of *Broken Pencil* magazine and co-founded *Spacing* magazine. Lindsay lives in Toronto, Ontario.